Operations Risk

Operations Risk

Managing a Key Component of Operations Risk under Basel II

David Loader

ELSEVIER

Amsterdam • Boston • Heidelberg • London
New York • Oxford • Paris • San Diego
San Francisco • Singapore • Sydney • Tokyo
Butterworth-Heinemann is an imprint of Elsevier

BH

Butterworth-Heinemann is an imprint of Elsevier
Linacre House, Jordan Hill, Oxford OX2 8DP, UK
30 Corporate Drive, Suite 400, Burlington, MA 01803, USA

First edition 2007

British Library Cataloguing in Publication Data
A catalogue record for this book is available from the British Library

Library of Congress Cataloging-in-Publication Data
A catalog record for this book is available from the Library of Congress

ISBN-13: 978-0-7506-6799-9
ISBN-10: 0-7506-6799-0

For information on all Butterworth-Heinemann publications
visit our web site at books.elsevier.com

Typeset by Integra Software Services Pvt. Ltd, Pondicherry, India
www.integra-india.com

Printed and bound in MPG Books Ltd. Bodmin, Cornwall, Gt. Britain

07 08 09 10 11 10 9 8 7 6 5 4 3 2 1

Contents

Introduction

Risk is an important subject in financial markets and of course our everyday lives, and yet it is sometimes easy to recognise risk and yet also sometimes very difficult.

In all the many initiatives, regulations and recommendations associated with financial markets we still primarily have three types of risk: market, credit and operational.

We have Basle II, Sarbannes–Oxley, various EU Directives and MiFID all of which relate to risk in various ways and yet in terms of operational risk it is the very fundamental processing, people and procedures that generate the risk scenarios and events. All the directives in the world will prevent credit-card fraud or Internet banking risks. Neither will they totally stop other frauds, money laundering or embarrassing "cock ups" that cause huge reputation and sometime financial loss.

Operations risk is often "lost" in the generic term 'operational risk', depending on the definition of "operational risk".

Operations is very much about management, people, projects, systems, processes and procedures and client service and so it is therefore reasonable to consider it to be at the very least a very significant part of operational risk.

For this very reason operations staff and managers are at the heart of most of the operational risk management process, although often they do not realise it. This is simply because by doing their jobs well they typically "manage" somewhere in the region 80% of the firms' operational risk. Risk managers must manage the remainder and do so in conjunction with the operations managers and teams be they in securities settlement, premises or technology.

In this book we look at the issues affecting the operations teams particularly in banking and investment businesses and give an insight into what the nature of operations and operational risk really is.

Whether you work in operations teams, audit or of course risk management, understanding operations risk is vitally important. In this book, I hope I have given a really good insight that will interest the reader and maybe help prevent them being part of the next huge "operational risk" event!

1

The operational risk universe

Operational risk is not new. Indeed it would be difficult to find many managers in banks and financial institutions who are not familiar with the term or with the phrase "Basel II"* or today MiFID**. However, whilst it is a fact that operational risk has been around as long as both market and credit risk, it is only comparatively recently that the financial services industry has truly recognised the risk presented in an "operational" environment.

Many would attribute the recognition of operational risk to the activities of organisations and individuals in the 1990s that led to a string of high profile financial disasters, notably the rogue trader Nick Leeson. However, that is too simplistic and many organisations were very much aware of the implications and impacts of strategic and process activities not being carried out efficiently and correctly long before Nick Leeson. In the 1970s, for instance, London-based market makers and brokers, deregulation had not at that stage created the all singing all dancing "investment bank", were looking at a very new product that had been successfully introduced into the United States. That product was financial derivatives, more precisely at that time, futures and options on bonds, interest rates, currencies and later equity indices and individual securities.

The pending introduction of these products into the London and European financial markets was causing considerable problems and

* The revised operational risk directive by the Basel Committee of the Bank for International Settlement.
** The Eu Markets in Financial Instruments Directive.

issues, not least concerning product knowledge, procedures, processes and of course systems. The only "experience" of these types of product lay with the firms involved in commodities. Bearing in mind that at that time technology was relatively a new product itself, and many processes that are today taken for granted as being highly automated were very much manual processes and therefore people-intensive and time-sensitive, the introduction of relatively sophisticated products was a major challenge and a significant risk event. With little product knowledge in the front office let alone the support functions, there was at the very least a steep learning curve for those people involved in the various related projects. As a result directors, partners, senior managers and so on were increasingly concerned at their dilemma, which was of course about how to safely manage these derivatives or to opt out of their use and maybe miss out on a highly profitable and successful new market.

It became apparent that there would be a very different scenario for virtually every organisation, and yet at the time risk events were not as formally or structurally recognised as they are today. Certainly, losses occurred in the market, credit and operational areas, and these were analysed to ascertain the causes, effects and remedial actions. In other words risk management.

However, there were various risk events developing elsewhere in the financial markets. There was for instance the change from physical settlement of transactions in shares and bonds, with information being disseminated in paper form, to automated settlement and later dematerialised (paperless) securities.

This change was not always smooth, and yet whilst we could say that the chance of a risk event manifesting itself was clearly higher during this period the ultimate outcome of a dematerialised settlement would be to reduce an operational risk that is settlement fails, delayed settlement and so on.

Another example of operational risk awareness would be the more recent changes in retail banking as the traditional high-street banking was supplemented by the advent of electronic banking, cash machines and a whole range of Internet-based savings and borrowing facilities. These fast and highly automated processes presented new risks of errors and problems that were very different from the practices that were very familiar to staff and managers in the branches.

Change and risk have long been recognised as inseparable. There is in most people and environment a natural dislike of change. The unknown is not, to most people, welcome and even those who say they embrace change often do so more from the thrill of the challenge than from a real desire for change. There are many reasons for this of course. Some are allied to concerns over job losses, others to the ability to understand a new procedure or process.

There is also often an irrational reaction to change with unjustified blame, massive distrust and even open hostility being displayed. People embracing change become the enemies of those opposing it. Force fields, something we will talk about later in the book, are created, which cause delay, disruption even sabotage, and so a change within a firm or a process creates a massive operational risk.

Of course it was not that new products or change were a new phenomena, you can check your history books to see that this is hardly a new thing as after all markets had been evolving all the time. Nor was it that they suddenly materialised as operational risk issues, far from it. The operational risk of a transaction had started when man made the very first "trade", whenever that might have been! But what these changes and challenges did do, given the nature and the extent of the changes to the existing environment, was to make managers and many staff more aware of how significant the changes were, and therefore how there was an increased risk of errors and problems as countless tasks and functions disappeared or changed and new skills needed to be learned and developed.

Whilst there was certainly an awareness of a heightened risk situation amongst operations and administration managers, it was still not accepted or recognised in most organisations at senior management level that the risk could be so severe that a business could be devastated by it. Also given the nature of the strategic thinking at the time, growth and change were embraced along with the inevitable operational losses, which became thought of as the cost of being in the business.

This thinking was fundamentally flawed because risk-generated losses were being put down as operational inefficiencies. There was no recognition that a combination of or high level of operational inefficiencies was a significant element of a highly dangerous risk situation for the firm concerned. This "cost" of the business was in most cases just accepted, and even accepted to the point that resource and investment levels in an operational environment were very much a secondary consideration with the focus firmly on the sharp end of the business. Here of course risk was very much recognised and both market and credit risk were taken very seriously.

So why was operational risk by and large ignored?

Well, the principal reason was that significant financial loss and to some extent reputation loss had not historically been seen as a result of operational failure. Big losses caused by failure to understand or control exposures to markets or counterparties were however known to have occurred and were often publicly documented. The risk was therefore very much upfront in the decision-making process related to trading and clients and/or counterparties and also in terms of investment in risk modelling and risk management. Even regulation was massively geared towards front office and sales and dealt with control over exposures and the market and credit risk issues facing firms.

What happened to cause the collapse of Barings Bank would change the thinking dramatically.

The case of Barings is perhaps the story of multiple failings in terms of risk awareness, controls, management and general professionalism. In many people's opinion there are still unanswered questions, and certainly in my own case a belief that there was far more behind what happened than has ever become public and probably will never become public.

To understand the impact that Barings had one would only need to look at the reaction of the regulators and financial organisations themselves. It is fair to say that in the immediate aftermath of the Barings collapse many senior managers were in somewhat of a blind panic. Questions were being fired at them from clients, regulators, non-executive directors and, if the manager was responsible for derivatives, from his colleagues in other business units. "Can this happen here?" was a fairly standard one whilst the real panic merchants were screaming "get out of derivatives now?"

Procedure reviews, systems reviews, personnel reviews, historical data; you name it and the request came in for it. Suddenly, operations were something everyone wanted to know about, controls and procedures were king and "who is responsible for operational risk" became the top item on the Board Meeting Agenda.

Meanwhile the regulators were in much the same state, unable to comprehend what had happened and how such failures of fundamental management could have occurred. The UK Government decided that the Bank of England could not be responsible for regulating the banks, and on the international front the Bank for International Settlement (BIS) decided this operational risk issue needed addressing and the Basel Committee was established.

Despite the significant changes taking place in financial markets and the growth of globalisation; despite the increasing complexity of products and reliance on technology, only when a rogue trader collapsed a bank did the world "discover" operational risk!

Post barings

After the initial hysteria, only when some truly appalling management decisions were made about operational risks that showed unbelievable lack of awareness of the true risk environment their businesses operated in, the financial markets came to terms, as it always does, with what had happened, why it had happened and how it had happened.

A realisation that operational risk existed, and had always existed, and that there was a need for some degree of operational risk management (ORM) was embraced by most organisations. Those with significant business in derivatives products naturally led the evolution of the management process and ORM became a key business issue. Many of these organisations found that in fact the operational risks they were facing were managed by the existing procedures and the performance of the managers and supervisors in the normal course of their responsibilities and work.

The procedures and process of ORM became extended to other elements of the securities and banking business as the skills and techniques developed.

Initially, it was assumed that many of the techniques that were used in the management of market and credit risk would be applied for operational risk. However, as the scope of the risk became ever wider it became apparent that this type of risk would be difficult to quantify and that much of the assessment and measurement of operational risk would inevitably be subjective.

Attention was drawn to how to quantify operational risk but many were still puzzled as to what exactly was the definition of operational risk? Confusion existed between "operations" risk and the wider context of operational risk, which included, amongst others, operations risk as a category. Some parties considered that operational risk encompassed everything that could not be included in market or credit risk.

This confusion was worrying. The risks associated with payments were fundamentally different than that concerning say building access. Both were operational risks but very different and yet also to some extent related. Could a payment be made if staff could not access the office? In the United Kingdom this was not such a key issue as, sadly, the effects of the terrorist activities by the Irish Republican Army (IRA) had meant that disaster recovery was a recognised requirement to mitigate against the disruption of business. Firms had secondary sites where their business could continue and even smaller organisations, where a full-blown disaster recovery site was not practical on cost grounds, nevertheless had contingencies in place should they be needed.

The influence of BIS

Risk management was evolving until the BIS decided that first operational risk needed to be defined and that secondly the systemic risk to the markets was such that banks and other financial organisations should set aside capital to mitigate the risk in much the same way that they did for market and credit risk, much of the development was very ad hoc. This is not to say that progress had not been made towards common standards. In addition to BIS, the British Bankers Association (BBA), the International Securities Services Association (ISSA), the Futures and Options Association, many other industry groups and the major consultancies were busy promoting discussion, issuing guidelines and consultative papers.

Conferences were devoted to the subject of operational risk, magazines on the subject appeared and within organisations operational risk groups, managers and committees were established. Middle offices became part of a risk-control process, and needless to say countless hours and copious amounts of money were flung at operational risk.

The operational risk pendulum swung from being business-related to regulatory-driven and then to the more central position of being both regulatory- and business-driven.

Operational risk management

Today, there is widespread recognition of the subject of operational risk and the need for operational risk management. The regulatory and business drivers behind ORM continue so that more added value is provided out of the need to address ORM. Techniques whilst still evolving are also mature and to some extent proven. Loss and incident data has been collected over several years and now forms a realistic and credible database for measurement and assessment. BIS has done much to encourage debate and discussion in areas like know your client (KYC), outsourcing, e-banking and so on. For organisations like fund managers there has been help, such as that given by The Futures and Options Association, which has published a Guide to The Risk of Derivatives for end-users, for complex but attractive products that are now more and more used. There is, or at least should be, less potential for a "Leeson" but the possibility has not been eradicated, it never will be given the fact that risk is an inherent part of many financial market businesses and the equally important fact that the core operational risk is about processes and people.

Operational risk is now sufficiently mature that within its ORM framework we can isolate categories of risk and they are significant enough in their own right to merit greater description.

Types of risk

One issue about operational risk that has evolved is the difficulty in distinguishing what is in fact operational risk and what is not.

Definitions do not always help in this, as for instance the Basel definition does not refer to the reputational loss possibility of a risk event happening. Also what is the risk implication of an error? Errors occur in virtually any type of process, the risk is therefore more complex than simply recognising an error. The issue is, was the error a single event or a repetitive event? But then again was it impacting elsewhere or was it contained? However, it could be that the error is inevitable, is recognised and is accepted as part of the business.

You get the gist? Operational risk is very diverse and is massively about perception and reality, something that is not always one and the same thing. A loss happening is not always a disaster. It may be undesirable and it will affect the profit/loss figures but it is not necessarily a threat to the business.

Traders make errors in their dealing, but if the result of those errors is the equivalent of say 1 per cent of the profit they make, how much of risk is it to the business?

As a firm knows traders make errors, they put in place adequate controls and procedures to ensure that the number, type and value of those errors is recorded and known.

However, if there is a failure in controls and procedures that are supposed to validate the trades and the resulting profit/losses then there is the significant risk that the 1 per cent figure is incorrect. If it is in fact 51 per cent then the trader is out of control and/or a liability and the firm is massively at risk.

What we can see is that trading errors, recognised as part of the business of the firm, can be a non-issue or equally a massive operational risk source.

That is what this book is all about so let us explore the *operations risk* element of operational risk.

> "Failure to adequately identify, evaluate and manage operational risks can expose the organisation, and the market itself, to financial loss . . ."
>
> *Chris Thompson, Jeff Thompson & John Garvey*
> *Global Custodian/Fall 1996*

2

Defining operations risk in investment and retail banking

Banking is a term that it can be said is no longer such a straightforward and obvious process. Most people associate banking with their own financial management and so the retail-banking sector of the financial markets is more widely recognised and understood than the banking activity that today we call investment banking.

We will come onto wholesale banking and investment banking later but let us first of all look at the operations risk in the retail sector.

Retail banking

In retail banking there are many potential operational risk scenarios and many of these are operations-related. The structure of retail banking today is very much a mix of "branch" style banking where there is direct personal contact, telephone banking and e-banking. Paper is still in evidence in many aspects of this type of banking service and this can be true even when we are looking at telephone and e-banking. In the area of business banking for small- and medium-size enterprises (SMEs), we again find a mix of automated and manual services.

In operational terms, the risks most likely to occur are within the processing and the customer contact areas. Failures in procedures will be the probable root cause of risk events and yet many banks operate on a basis of fairly autonomous yet very much interlinked structures, where there may be both unique and common procedures in operation.

It is interesting to look at the risks that banks themselves consider they are facing.

- Confidentiality of client data
- Payment processes
- Compliance failure
- Reliance on services and products from other areas of the bank
- Change management
- Controls failure
- Inefficient processes
- Relationship dangers
- Fraud (internal and external).

In retail banking like all organisations, operations risks can be looked at in a number of ways.

Catastrophic risks – Clearly there are events that have occurred that can be described as "catastrophic", that is the collapse of Barings Bank or Allfirst which have been attributable in whole or in part to operational failures.

There are "Generic risks" like credit card frauds and regulatory review of the sales process, where there is little or no ability for an organisation to mitigate against all risks as they may not have total or sufficient control over the situation.

Unique risks – Then there is the operations risk that is created internally by the bank. This would cover headline areas like resource levels, skill sets and even the operational structure itself including management.

Creeping risk – An example might be problems with fees and charges that originate in one area of the bank but manifest themselves in another, usually with greater severity, that is a client is debited the wrong charges that could lead to compensation and also a regulatory situation.

Managing operations risk in retail banking

In any organisation there is some degree of ORM simply because employees do their tasks correctly. Without active management and leadership, however, that organisation is both vulnerable if task-performance levels deteriorate and is missing the benefits that active ORM can bring.

From my experience, ORM does not just happen, it has to be nurtured and developed. It also has to be meaningful, focussed and above all deliver value to the bank.

Too much "ORM" and it will be expensive for the business, difficult to implement and will result in few, if any, benefits for the bank, too little "ORM" and the business can suffer and possibly be in extreme danger.

As in every case of risk management, the structure of the organisation is a key consideration and the risk management structure needs to complement it. In most retail banks there are several business units. Each will have unique risks and common risks. It is crucial that the operations risk is apparent within a business unit and across business units.

Consider the somewhat simplistic and hypothetical structure below. Although not necessarily a structure that one might be totally familiar with, it nevertheless serves its purpose in showing how the business units are interoperable in risk terms and also silo based in risk terms.

It is important to stress that whilst in Figure 2.1 risk management "sits" above the business areas, in no way should the assumption be made that the business reports to ORM. However, what a successful ORM structure will deliver is to create a risk-awareness culture across the business areas and to act as a conduit for identification, monitoring

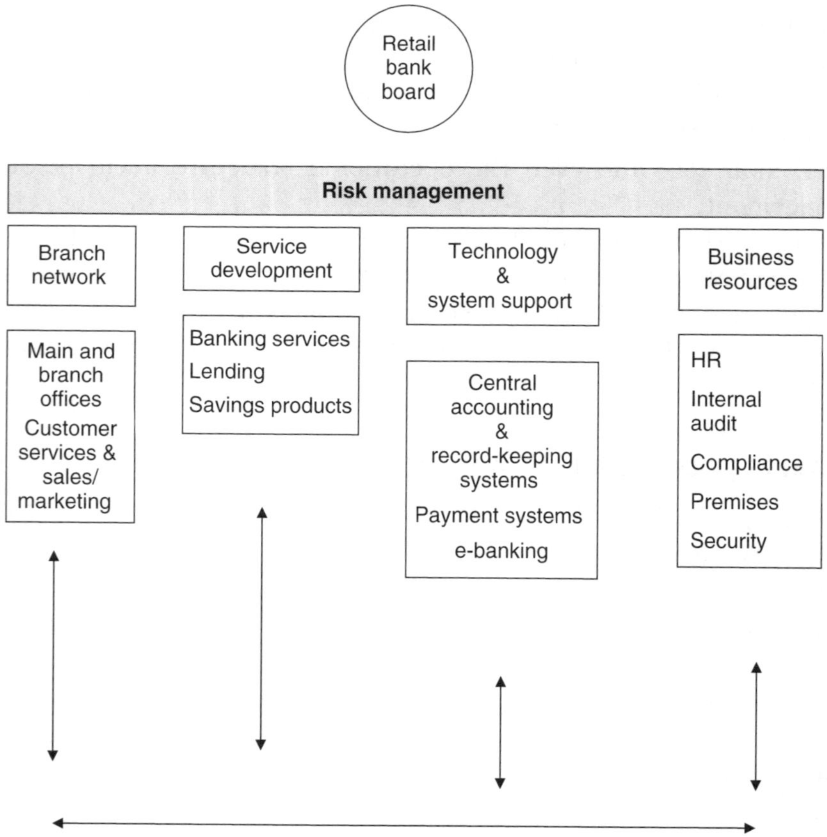

Figure 2.1 Risk Management Structure

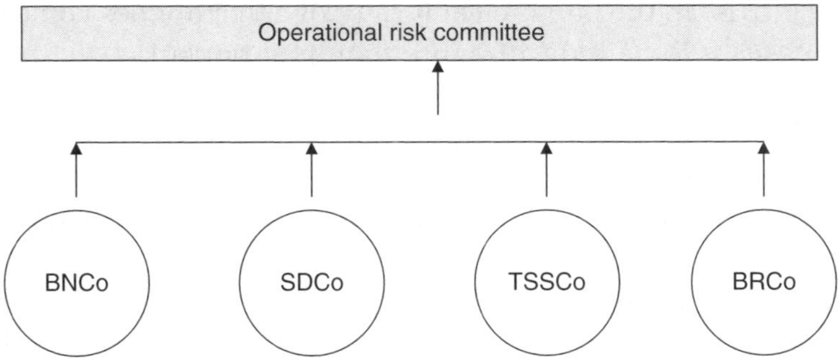

Figure 2.2 Operational Risk Committee Relationships with Business

and control of risks related to a business unit and across business units.

One successful method of coordinating this effectively is to create a system of managing the group-wide risk through a system of committees responsible for risk within the business units, which in turn feed into the operational risk committee (ORCo).

Within this ORCo the exchange of data on risks, controls and so on enables the diverse risk of a diverse banking function to be consolidated into a risk profile that can then be addressed within the scope and appetite of the group for risk (Figure 2.2).

The ORCo receives the risk assessment from each business unit committee in a standard format so that the self-assessment techniques can be standardised and related across the business through mapping. Likewise, controls can be devised that are both specific and also generic or common across the group. Given the nature of retail banking this flexibility between standardised and bespoke risk assessment and control process is crucially important.

Types of operations risk affecting retail banks

Clearly, retail banking has a high profile with its customers and at the same time there is still some kind of aura around a bank. It is perceived as "safe", reliable", "protective", and, if you believe some of the sales pitches, the individual's "very unique and personal" banking arrangement.

In essence, customers of a bank do not expect any nasty surprises and certainly they do not expect anything to happen that would suggest the "comfort" feeling is misplaced. An error on their personal account is therefore viewed with horror, that is assuming of course that they check their account in the first place. Many do not because they have an implicit trust in the bank to get it right. If an error does come to light in these cases it is viewed with more than just horror!

Customer account errors

The misrouting of an item to a customer's account can occur for a variety of reasons, but a failure in the control process must have occurred. Equally, the application of incorrect charges shows a failure to verify the amount before posting. The reasons for this often lie in the automation of the process so that if an error occurs it is likely that the statement is on its way to or has arrived at the customer. In many cases the "error" is not actually identified by the bank until the customer complains.

The issue for the bank is now whether the error is applicable to that single account or is it systemic and affecting many or all accounts.

The response to the situation is critically important. The customer needs placating. The extent of the problem needs identifying. A decision on the action to be taken is needed.

Example

A customer is debited with a charge for a currency transaction that has not taken place.

Immediate observations

- How could this have happened?
- What is needed to reverse the charge?
- Has the customer suffered any costs/loss?
- Has/will the customer make a formal complaint?
- How will the matter be dealt with in terms of
  - the customer?
  - internal investigation?
  - compensation?
  - regulatory?
- What is the operational risk impact?
- What damage limitation exercise needs to happen?

Possible outcomes

The reason for the incorrect application of a charge to the account would be associated with either a manual process error or a system problem.

If it is a manual keying error then the verification control process has not worked.

If it is system generated there could be corruption in the database.

> In either case the operations risk is that this is not confined to this single error and further errors may have happened and not been recognised or will happen in the future.

Action

The customer

Obviously, if the client has suffered a loss or cost, as they will have done in this case, it must be rectified. The amount erroneously debited must be re-credited along with any interest lost as a result of the amounted debited from the account or indeed any interest charged on an overdrawn balance.

The re-crediting process should be overseen by a manager/supervisor (an incorrect re-credit would compound the problem!)

If a formal complaint has been made by the customer a full internal investigation must be made and a reply provided to the customer, including any offer of compensation and the customers right and route to take the complaint further if not satisfied with the response from the bank.

Risk impact

In order to establish the extent of the impact of the risk it is imperative to analyse whether:

- The process was automated or manual
- Was it client-specific or an automatic charge process applied on as a batch process across many clients
- It is the first time the charge or a similar charge has been made
- Previous charges were applied correctly
- Controls failed and the cause of the failure
- A regulatory report needs to be prepared.

Damage limitation and preventative action

Operations and process managers must:

- Carry out a review of transaction charges and errors on such charges over a suitable period (say 6 or 12 months)
- Review the effectiveness and relevance of all the procedures for charging fees to accounts

- Confirm the verification processes are robust
- Ensure the reconciliation of transaction charges to transactions is thorough and effective
- Reconfirm the self-assessment techniques are adequate and will identify this type of risk scenario
- Document any weaknesses found and the actions taken to rectify the weakness.

Managing other operations risks

Sales and marketing

One area that has a high-risk profile is sales and marketing.

Most people are aware of the issues that have surrounded the so-called 'miss selling' of endowment products and pensions. In both cases, there were issues about whether the full implications of how the product might perform that were not explained sufficiently or even at all. The result being that when equity markets declined significantly and for a long period the performance of the investments was such that they would not, in many cases, meet the returns expected or in the case of endowments the return needed to pay off the mortgage they were supposed to cover.

Clearly, the launch of any product must be not only successful but also compliant with regulatory standards and rules applicable to the type of product, the bank and its customers.

For instance, there are specific rules related to investment products that require the marketing materials to be constructed in such a way that they can be understood by the prospective investor.

Material that includes facts is fine, however where facts are "doctored" to make the product look better would be unacceptable. The operations risk here would be that the people either compiling the material or checking the compilation have not completed the task correctly.

These are just a few examples of operations risk in retail banking. There are others and these are illustrated with some case studies which can be researched by visiting banking association websites and reviewing articles on, for instance, the collapse of BCCI.

Risk in Investment Banking

Much of this book is related to the operations risk likely to be found in investment banking, so a brief introduction is all that is needed here.

Principal operational and operations risks in investment banking concern:

- Structure of the investment bank
- Extent of global market coverage, activity and client base
- The complexities of the products, processes and procedures employed
- Extent, age and level of technology available across the business
- The competency of the management and personnel
- The direction of the senior management.

As an investment bank is a very complex business, the operations functions are also highly complex and can be aligned on a business basis i.e. silo or across the businesses in a single operational function of division.

A generic example of the structure in a global investment bank can be found in Appendix 5.

It is worth noting here that in my experience most operational risk in investment banking is usually related to one or more of the following:

- Resource levels in comparison to the activity
- Skill sets in management and staff
- Technology issues
- Outdated and ineffective procedures
- Problems with outsourced work and third parties
- Lack of controls over processes
- Stress and working environment

3

Operations risk

For convenience, operational risk can be divided into various categories. Organisations are of course very different in their structure and so the categories that are used will be bespoke. That said there are some generic headings that are fairly common, for instance Legal, Technology and Human Resources. Included in these generic headings would be Operations Risk.

Operations risk can then be further categorised into sub-headings and examples of these might be Settlement, Systems, Custody, and so on. There will also often be sub-headings that are the same as the general categories and so for instance we can have Legal as a sub-heading for the Operations Risk category.

What is the point of these categories and sub-headings?

Operational risk is a fluid risk that contains elements of four types of risk: *catastrophic, creeping, generic* and *specific*. As the characteristic and extent of the impact of a risk is by nature extremely difficult to fully map, the use of categories and sub-headings enables a big picture of the different risks and total risk to be built up, as we will see later in the book. The operational-risk profile changes constantly as factors such as the strategic aims of the business, the activity and the structure of the business themselves change. It is important to be able to see how and where the change to the risk profile is happening if dynamic and successful risk management is to be achieved. By monitoring and analysing the profile of categories and sub-headings, that change as data and management information is recorded, the operational managers and risk managers can take relevant actions to control the enterprise-wide risk (Figure 3.1).

Operations risk will, in most cases, comprise the risk associated with process flows, procedures, transaction completion (settlement) and the people and systems that perform and manage these tasks. In financial

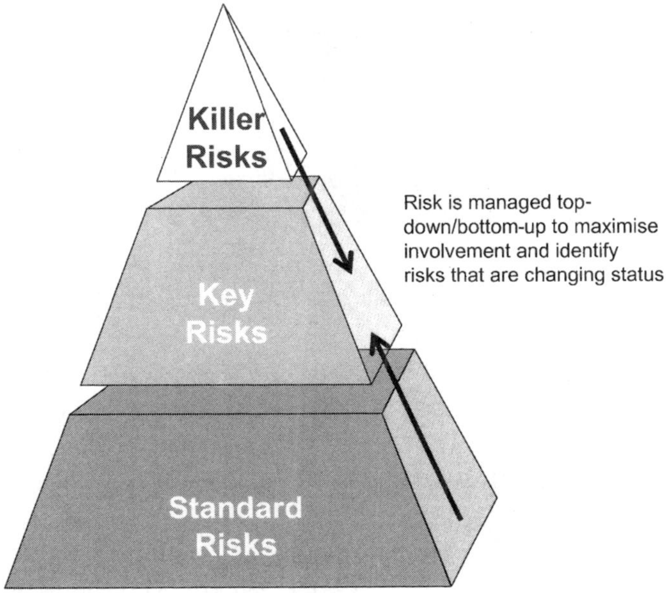

Figure 3.1 Enterprise-wide Risk Pyramid

markets this will include the processes from pre-trade to post-trade and on to final settlement and custody plus the structure that is in place to facilitate this. It is evident that the operations risk element is intrinsically linked to the type of activity undertaken by the organisation as well as the complexity and level of activity. The geographical structure and business profile plus the client base will also have a significant bearing on the type of risk situations that will be possible. Technology is clearly a major influence in terms of risk types and levels.

Operations Risk therefore has sub-sections which could look something like that shown in Figure 3.2.

Transaction capture	Controls
Money laundering & fraud	Client service
Cash management	Personnel
Third-party supplier risks	Reconciliations
Business continuity	Reporting
Compliance	Settlement

Figure 3.2 Operations Risk Headings

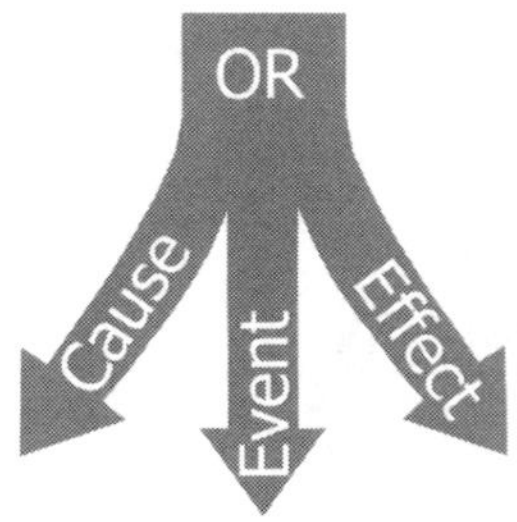

Figure 3.3 Operational Risk Components

As is common with the whole operational risk environment there are three central considerations: the risk event, the cause and the impact (Figure 3.3).

In operations terms this is easy to illustrate, for instance a failure to send a correct settlement instruction will potentially cause a settlement fail, which in turn could result in a market claim. Thus we have the risk event, the settlement fail; the cause, the incorrect instruction; and the impact, the market claim as shown in Figure 3.4.

There are two points to note here. First, the actual risk event may have occurred or may be a "near miss", and secondly there may be more than one event, cause and impact. This is important to understand and recognise if we are to be successful in the management of operations risk.

When we then consider what sub-headings there are for operations risk, we need to use the template that was described in Chapter 1 to identify those key risk causes within the environment. Operations functions are subject to a considerable number and diversity of processes and therefore it is reasonable to assume that there will be a significant number of risks.

Once again we can look to categorise these so that we can better analyse the types of risk and produce the effective risk controls.

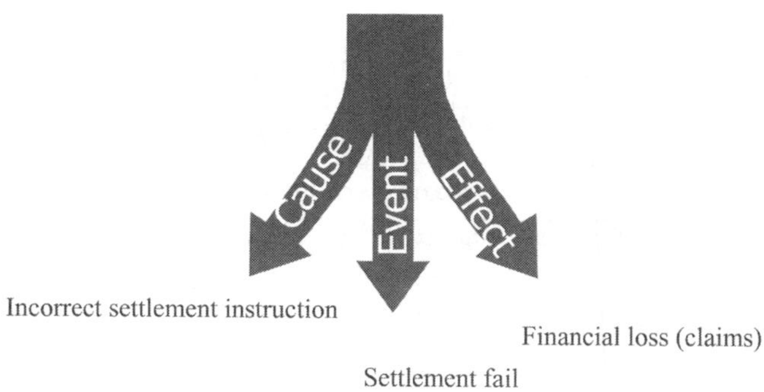

Figure 3.4 Event Components

In a securities operation, for instance, the sub-headings for subsections of operations risk might be:

- Trade capture
- Trade processing
- Reconciliation
- Customer service
- Regulatory
- Technology
- People
- Management
- Counterparts

Then within each of these headings we can further categorise by, for instance, geographical location, product type and so on, so that we have something that looks like that shown in Figure 3.5.

We have now created a risk picture by using what is often referred to as "risk envelopes" or "boxes". Into these "envelopes" we can insert the possible risk event types that are considered by the managers and supervisors to be of sufficient importance to be included. We are therefore creating not only a relatively comprehensive picture but we are doing so through a process of identifying the main or key risks.

Analysing the risk value

If we are to have a risk management process that is meaningful and adds value to the business, the types of risk identified must be risks and not for instance just errors or situations that have little or no significant impact. The danger is of course that a situation may appear to be innocuous and indeed in a particular process or function that may well be the case, but that same situation may have a much greater impact elsewhere in the organisation or indeed in operations.

The value of the risk situation is therefore the significance of the impact and distribution of the impact. If we assign a measure to each of say 0 to 10 then we can unscientifically at least create a matrix of the value of the identified risks. In turn we can then apportion these risks into *standard risks*, *key risks* and *killer risks*.

Operations risk needs to be carefully looked at in terms of what constitutes a standard, key or killer risk.

The fundamental assumption about operations risk is that it stems from processes.

Those processes are reflected in Figure 3.6.

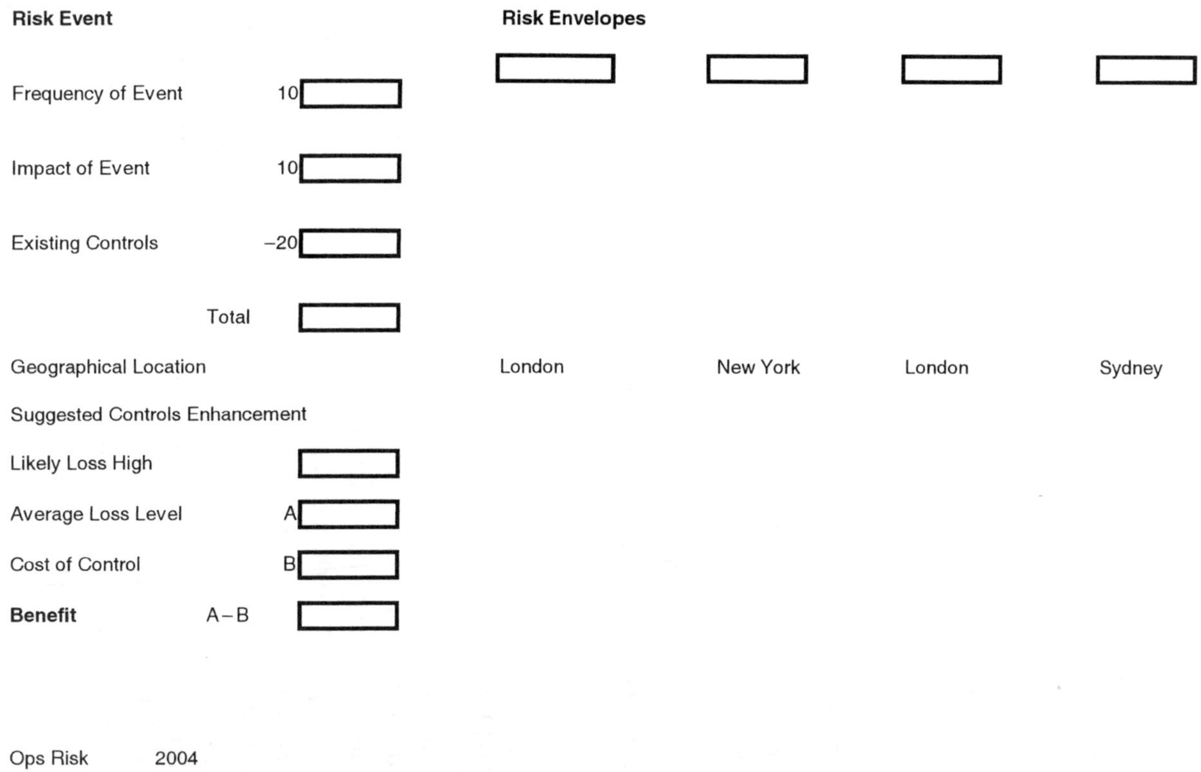

Figure 3.5 Operational Risk Scorecard

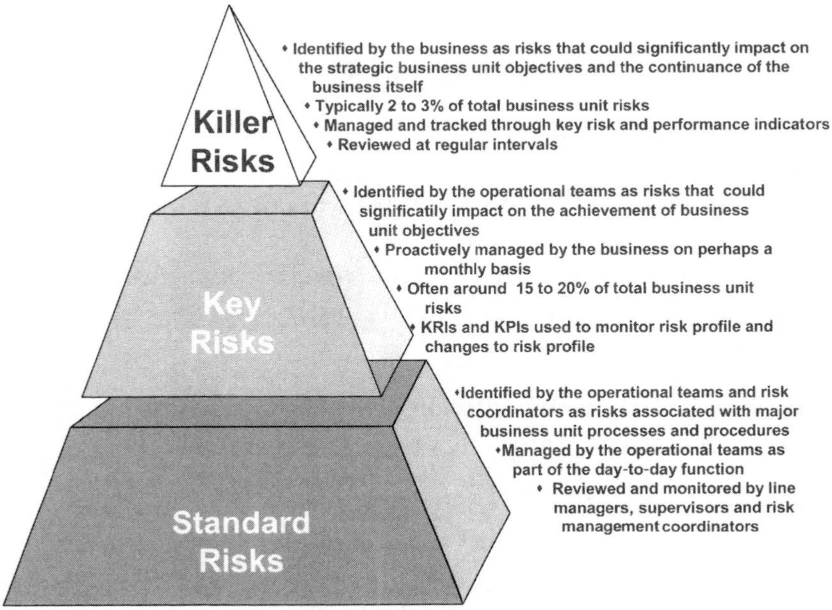

Figure 3.6 Risk Pyramid Management

Standard risks are those that are permanently in existence and are part of the core processes that a firm is using on a continuous basis. In most cases, the teams and supervisors responsible for the functions related to the processes manage these potential risks. There are associated or linked risks that also need to be identified. For instance, the technology risks associated with the process may be identified as a key or even killer risk. The table below illustrates the links.

Process path	Trade capture	Trade reconciliation	Posting	Reporting
Standard Risk	Incorrect client code			
Key risk	→	Error missed in reconciliation	Wrong client code not noticed	
Killer risk			⟶	Client statement sent to wrong person

In the above example, the killer risk is the huge reputational damage done by sending a client the totally wrong information that in fact belongs to some other client.

Summary of operations risk

Let us remind ourselves what the objective of risk management is:

1. Identify what the risks are
2. Know the frequency of occurrence of the risk
3. Understand how and where the risk will potentially impact
4. Measure the impact of the risk
5. Introduce the controls that will manage the risk within the framework of the regulatory requirements and the risk appetite and policy of the business.

So let us now look at the different elements of risk and see how that impacts on operations teams.

Market risk

The operations manager is involved in market risk, not specifically because of trading decisions and strategies but because of the by-products of the dealing. This involves not only the clearing, settlement and accounting for the products but also the characteristics of the products. In fact, each of the following needs to be totally understood so that a risk profile or universe can be established:

- The characteristics of the product(s) used
- The market structure
- The country(ies)'s risk profile for the products traded
- The clearing and settlement structure
- The regulatory and tax environments
- The accounting issues.

We need to analyse these further.

Characteristics

In general terms, products tend to be classified as either "vanilla" or "exotic", the former being fairly standard in its composition and the latter more complex. There are many simple examples like, for instance, a fixed income "bullet" bond and a convertible bond or a standardised exchange-traded call option and an over-the-counter average rate Asian option.

Each product has a different process associated with it because in the one case there is a predetermined outcome or a right to decide on an outcome and in the other there is a variable outcome and/or need for a decision.

The resultant process flows must reflect this. If they do not then the risks increase and the likelihood of a risk event occurring also increases.

Management risk

Managing risk is fundamental to the banking and securities business. Managers represent a risk in so much as their failure to perform damages the business and places the business at significant operational and operations risk. Consider the following which are both directly the responsibility of the manger:

Inadequate procedures and controls

If a financial institution does not have written procedures and clearly defined organisational charts, it is easy for processes to be missed. These problems are aggravated if there are frequent organisational or process changes.

Information or reporting risk

Information or reporting risk is the risk that the reports and sources of information that management use to make their decisions contain incorrect or misleading information. Incorrect and misleading information can lead management to make wrong policy decisions and to make corrective action in the wrong direction. Misleading, distorted or delayed information can lead to trends or mistakes not being identified and, thus, ignored. Badly produced reports can lead to the incorrect amount of client money being segregated.

In both the above cases the manager directly influences the way in which the processes and procedures are devised and implemented for the functions.

There are of course other specific risks faced by financial institutions as we will see throughout the book. These include the following.

Market or principal risk

Market risk is the risk that changes in market conditions will have a negative impact on an institution's profitability. Example of changing market conditions include changes in:

- Interest rates, referred to as interest rate risk
- Foreign exchange rates, referred to as foreign exchange risk or currency risk

- The market value of investments held by the institution, which is sometimes referred to as price risk or equity position risk (in the case of equities).

Factors affecting market risk are:

- The longer the position is held there is a greater possibility of an adverse market price movement.
- The liquidity or ease of resale when the level of risk becomes unacceptable for the holder. The longer it takes to find a buyer/seller the greater the risk of price movement.
- The volatility of price fluctuations. Some emerging market equities have fluctuating prices whereas many gilts have relatively stable prices.
- The sensitivity of the price to underlying factors. Derivatives prices move far quicker than the price of the underlying equity.

To evaluate its exposure to market risks, it is accepted that a financial institution should evaluate the market value of its positions daily. Financial institutions should also compare this exposure to established market risk limits. Market risk is often measured and monitored by value at risk (VAR) models that use probability-based methodologies to measure the institution's potential loss under certain market conditions. Value at risk is a statistical measurement of the maximum likely loss on a portfolio due to adverse market price movements. It calculates the loss if the price moves by two standard deviations or 95 per cent. It uses historical price movements to identify the probability of future adverse price movements. Another method is stress testing, which involves the application of extreme market movements that may arise as a result of hypothetical political or economic upheavals to a portfolio of investments.

'Mark to market' of all short positions at the bid price and all long positions at the offer price will enable a firm to ascertain its daily profit or loss. The mark to market value can be refined to take account of liquidity or settlement risk. Sensitivity analysis measures the degree to which the value of trading positions are vulnerable to changes in interest rates. Every future cash flow is discounted by the time value of money to give a net present value. The sensitivity calculation is usually expressed as the change in net present value of the portfolio produced by a one basis point movement in interest rates across the whole cash flow portfolio.

Credit or counterparty risk

Credit risk is the risk that a customer will fail to complete a financial transaction according to the terms of the contract, resulting in a loss to the financial institution. In general terms, credit ratings are used in assessing the suitability of a counterparty and in most larger organisations a specialist credit department will deal with this.

Firms need to measure their credit risk and compare their exposure to predetermined counterparty limits. Credit risk measurements should reflect the impact of changing market conditions on the current and future ability of customers to meet contractual obligations. The evaluation of customer and counterparty creditworthiness, as well as the setting of individual credit limits, should be the responsibility of an independent credit department.

However, there is another type of counterparty risk.

It is also the possibility or probability that the operational performance of the client or counterparty will be sub-standard, and will therefore impact negatively on the firm's own performance. Typically, this will include repeated late settlement or payments, error-strewn instructions and so on. This can also be included under settlement risk.

Operational risk

It does no harm to define risk and sometimes to look at different definitions or even the same definition from another angle.

> **Definition**
>
> Operational risk is defined as 'the risk associated with human error, systems failures and inadequate procedures and controls during the processing of business related transactions and the loss of reputation by a failure to implement the processing correctly'. Operational risk can be broken down into further sub-sections like operations risk, technology risk, reporting risk, malicious risk, legal risk, regulatory risk and so on.

There are many types of operations risks including, but not restricted to:

- Settlement risk
- Personnel/HR risk

- Liquidity risk
- Financial risk
- Technology/system risk
- Legal risk
- Regulatory risk
- Reputation risk
- Cross border risk
- Custody risk.

Settlement risk is a sub-section of operational risk and relates to risks occurring within the settlement cycle. It is the risk that the transaction will not settle properly, that there will be a delivery of 'bad' stock, a late settlement or one counterparty will default on their obligation (this is also a credit risk). Settlement risk is greatest in free of payment deliveries and foreign exchange transactions. With foreign exchange transactions, there is a risk of non-receipt of the purchased currency after irrevocable instructions have been passed to deliver the sold currency. Banks operating in different time zones and over public holidays and weekends further exacerbate this problem. Developments like CLS Bank are designed to overcome the problem in Foreign Exchange (FX) markets.

Settlement risk is increased or decreased depending on the format of the clearing process. The Central clearing counterparty (CCP) concept where the clearing house becomes the counterparty to the trade significantly reduces the counterparty risk, whilst the "traditional" securities clearing process where counterparties remain linked until settlement causes potential problems notably the risk of settlement failure. Also, there can be the 'chain effect' as there are frequently many interdependent transactions. For example, Figure 3.7 shows several transactions in TopStock that have become interdependent on each other but in the process have become "locked".

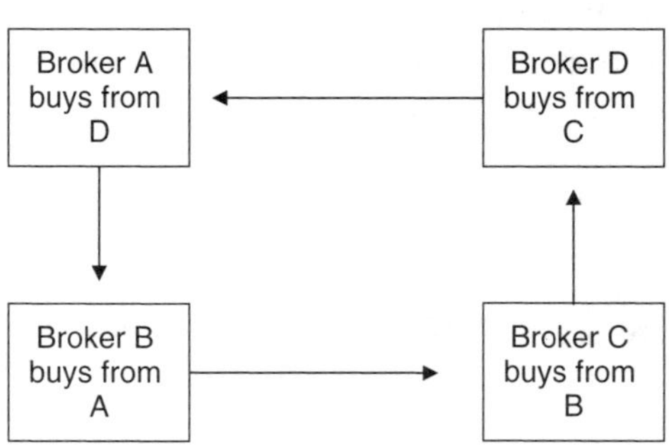

Figure 3.7 Illustration of a "Locked" Settlement Situation

Some clearing houses have procedures to overcome this locking or settlement circle situation. For instance, CREST runs a 'circles' algorithm to resolve inter-dependencies.

Means of reducing settlement risk

There are several basic ways in which settlement risk can be mitigated.

As with all risk there is a need for extensive knowledge of:

- Products
- Market and clearing structure
- Settlement processes
- Payment processes
- Custodial processes
- System capabilities.

There must also be an awareness of the effectiveness of the internal procedures and processes, how effective the controls are, and what potential developments and so on will impact positively and negatively on the risk position in the operations function.

One effective control over settlement risk is to ensure that DVP settlement should be used as often as possible and in the case of collateral and so on, delivery versus delivery. Although free of payment settlement is inevitable in some circumstances, the controls over this should be such that this is authorised and monitored at all times.

As mentioned earlier, today counterparty and settlement risk is further mitigated by the introduction of the Central Clearing Counterparty (CCP) for securities settlement. It is important to understand the concept of CCP and how its introduction and the role of the CCP will impact on the operational workflow. The appendices have details of relevant papers and so on pertaining to this.

Personnel/HR risk

People are one of a firm's biggest assets; they are also a very substantial source of risk.

Why is this so?

Essentially, the involvement of people at various stages in the operations cycle leads to inevitable situations where the individual, or indeed team performance, may be less than adequate to alleviate risk. Such a scenario would be the level of resource available to meet a volume of business. Another would be the product awareness of individuals involved in key stages of the process. Whatever the reason, and often the reasons for problems with personnel can be very difficult to manage, there is a risk like, for instance, the simple, but potentially highly dangerous human error. Examples of human error include inputting trade details incorrectly, for example a buy rather than a sell, 10 rather than 100, entering trades twice, running reports at the wrong time, forgetting to start IT processes and failing to back up data.

> A common enough phrase that is used in operations, and is frequently so true is:
> 'What can go wrong, will go wrong'

Human error is exacerbated by over-stretched staff in periods of high volume, staff absence due to illness and holidays, inexperienced staff and lack of clear written procedures. The latter is dealt with further in Chapter 8 and managing people in Chapter 6.

Liquidity risk

Liquidity risk encompasses two risks – one that might be defined as a market risk, the other operational. First, it is the risk of not being able to sell or buy a security at a given time or at an acceptable price. This may be because of a lack of market participants (a thin market) or due to technical or operational disruptions in the market place. A prime example would be a stock market crash with investors and institutions curtailing activity until volatility in the price of securities has reduced or a sustained "bull" run when there are many more buyers than sellers of stock.

Secondly, there is also funding liquidity risk that relates to a firm's cash flow or asset position. If cash flow is insufficient to meet its payment obligations on settlement dates or margin calls, a firm will have very major problems. There are many implications.

In a CCP environment, the failure to settle may constitute a default with the clearing house. Alternatively, the firm will be hit with claims or fines or both for failing to settle. In risk terms, one party's funding or asset liquidity risk is another party's counterparty risk.

Ultimately, Barings collapsed because they could not meet the margin calls on the Singapore Exchange for the derivatives positions that had grown to massive amounts as the Kobi earthquakes made the futures price move unfavourably. Management in Barings not knowing the true extent of the positions and not verifying why so much capital was required compounded the whole situation.

The collapse of Barings was managed by the clearing house and the markets, but the impact could have been far more extensive than it was, although many firms experienced huge liquidity problems in funding and trading as banks reduced lending facilities and credit departments reviewed their exposure to counterparties immediately after Barings demise. What everyone was concerned about was the possibility of other firms collapsing, referred to as 'systemic risk'.

Systemic risk

As with most types of risk systemic risk has a variety of formats. It is the ultimate liquidity risk whereby the default by one firm will cause further firms to default leading to further firms defaulting until the whole system collapses like a set of dominoes, for example the Wall Street Crash 1929. It is fear of the domino effect that causes the regulators, central banks and politicians to decide whether to step in to save firms or let them collapse. In the case of Barings and Long Term Capital Management (LTCM) the decisions were different because the impact of the collapse of LTCM was much more likely to precipitate a global collapse in the financial markets.

However, systemic risk also occurs within a firm and within an operations function. The principle is the same. A problem starts in one part of the firm or operations area and quickly impacts on other parts. An example would be problems with trade input or prices affecting the data sent to clients.

Risk rarely remains confined to one specific area or category and is therefore fluid. A risk may arise in one area but its severe impact may be felt in another. Thus the ability of the Operations Manager to identify source, cause and impact of operational risk is vitally important in the overall risk management process. An uncontrolled "linked" risk can ultimately create a disaster by becoming systemic and impacting elsewhere in an organisation.

Barings is an example of this where the failure to deal with operational risk issues like segregation of duties, reconciliations and payment validation ultimately led to the bank going bust.

In global operations there is a likelihood that standards and practices may vary across different parts of an organisation. Controls and procedures must be robust enough to recognise this.

Being able to understand the impact of a risk within a firm and within the operations area is a crucial role for the operations manager. Devising methods to measure the impact of risk, like "risk envelopes or portfolios" is vital.

Financial or treasury risk

In operations terms this is the inefficient use of cash and securities. Securities financing is covered in the next chapter but financial risk is also about penalties like fines, claims, overdraft costs, lack of control over expenditure particularly expenses, consumables and so on. We must also consider the loss that can occur by failing to make claims when we are the injured party or are entitled to benefits and so on.

Operations is a business and will have a budget. The manager must be able to prepare and control that budget effectively.

Technology risk

Technology is both power and danger. It gives advantages that can be exploited and problems that can be devastating. It drives operations but can equally be a constraint and it can be costly if not managed correctly.

Of all the things that affect operations performance, technology is the biggest friend and at the same time a potential nightmare. Only the managers who embrace technology and have the vision to develop it will be prepared for the changes and challenges that operations face in the coming years. Technology drives businesses, operations managers drive technology. Making it happen is the challenge for managers in both operations and technology. Technology risk is, not surprisingly, varied.

System failures

IT and system problems can range between problems with programs, for example system affected by viruses or bugs or incorrect codes to complete system failures when no trades can be input or processes can be run. IT problems are aggravated by either new systems that experience teething problems or old systems that have problems coping with the volumes and complexity of the business. IT problems are worsened if a financial institution has many different systems and applications bolting on to one another.

Technology awareness

How often is the term "it's a system problem" used? Perhaps, that should be supplemented by "how many times is it actually a systems problem"!

One critically important goal for operations and technology managers has to be making the staff in their respective areas understand the roles, capabilities, issues and opportunities each area offers. Only if there is a good understanding of how operations functions and how IT projects are managed and delivered will a really beneficial working relationship be established.

We consider the relationship between operations and technology in Chapter 7.

Legal risk

Legal risk is the risk that contracts are not legally enforceable (*ultra vires*) or documented incorrectly, leading to a loss for the firm. An example of this would be Hammersmith Council and the interest rate swap saga, where the council did not have the legal and necessary regulatory authority to engage in those transactions and thus the banks that were counterparty to the transactions had to suffer the loss.

Legal risk is linked to operations because of the many agreements that will exist between the firm and the counterparties. These agreements must be capable of protecting the firm in the case of disputes and problems at some stage in the relationship.

Typical agreements will be:

- Service Level Agreements
- Stock Lending Agreements
- Prime Brokerage/Clearing Agreements
- Custody Agreements
- Client Agreements
- Derivatives Agreements (either clearing or client i.e. ISDA documentation).

Operations will be liaising with the legal department in all these cases, but managers must be aware of the contents of the agreements and how this impacts on the function and the services provided and/or used.

Regulatory risk

Regulatory risk is the risk that a firm breaches the regulator's rules or codes of conduct:

In the United Kingdom, the Conduct of Business (COB) rules set out amongst other things how to classify customers and thus what investments are suitable. The COB rules set the content of customer agreement letter and contract notes, the content of advertising and so on. The client money and safe custody rules set out how client money must be segregated and separately identified at all times. Segregated money is held 'in trust' and due to the trust rules, the exact client money must be segregated. The financial resources rules set out how much capital buffer an institution must have to protect it from unforeseeable losses. The money laundering regulations set out what steps a financial institution must undertake to prevent and identify money laundering, and there are severe penalties for not complying with the procedures.

Reputation risk

Reputational risk is more important than people frequently realise and can easily lead to the rapid decline of a company. Examples of this are Andersen in the aftermath of Enron, Ratners following the Chairman's speech rubbishing the company's products and so on. This is particularly the case with companies having strong brand names, highly competitive markets or new up- and -coming companies like the Internet stockbroking companies.

A single error, ill-judged comment, slipping performance standards and service delivery or a period of repetitive problems can undo years of building the reputation.

Operations is at the front of the risk simply because it not only interfaces with external parties but also generates much of the critical administrative work associated with a firm like payments, information distribution and so on that performance is benchmarked to.

Instilling the danger of reputation risk into the minds of the operations team is crucial and the message needs constant reinforcing. Setting internal standards for the team, monitoring and then providing the analysis to them can achieve this. In this way the team are not only aware of their performance but can also provide input to maintaining and increasing standards.

Other risks

There are several other types of risk that the operations manager must be aware of.

Malicious risk

All companies face the risk of fraud and theft, of malicious intervention of the firm's systems by both employees, disgruntled ex-employees, competitors and outsiders. There are also an increasing number of computer hackers and other outsiders who may seek to ruin a company.

This is further evidenced by demonstrations such as the environmentalists and the "Stop The City" demonstrations that hit cities such as London, Seattle and so on.

Country risk

International investment and trading portfolios will carry numerous products that provide good opportunities for profit that may be issued and traded in emerging markets or markets where volatility is high. Emerging market or country risk is an important issue as there are likely to be heightened risk implications, particularly for operations.

These risks will typically be:

- Market open to manipulation
- Rapid expansion of newly listed securities caused by the dash for growth
- Volatile trading activity
- Conflicting and ineffective (by mature market standards) regulatory environment and structures
- Lack of and poor quality information
- Physical share certificates
- Lack of automated settlement processes
- Fraud
- Low liquidity
- Limited number of counterparties offering custody and other services.

Given that the emerging markets do present trading and investment opportunities, it is inevitable that operations teams must overcome the settlement problems associated with such business. To achieve this operations managers must familiarise themselves with the potential risks associated with each country and implement the necessary processes and controls to manage such business efficiently and safely. An example of the kind of problem that might arise is the action taken by Malaysia to protect its currency from speculators. By freezing any movement of capital from the country, profits on speculative investment and trading were effectively frozen and also at risk from any fluctuation in the value of the Ringett.

Understanding risk

The best way to understand risks is look at articles and reports on the major problems and events that have occurred in the industry and relate these to the business that you are involved in. Consider why things went wrong and how it could have been prevented and to what extent these were market, credit or operational risk (or any combination). Do your existing controls look strong enough to deal with such situations, particularly given the numerous changes taking place in the markets? Also it is important to look at past internal problems and how these have been resolved.

Some of the major risk-related industry events include Barings, the copper scandal at Sumitomo, star traders at Kidder Peabody, Morgan Grenfell, the Hammersmith and Fulham Local Authority interest rate swaps debacle and the problems over the default of Griffin.

Operations management

Finally, we must look at the risk that is posed by operations management. If we assume that operations management is about the day-to-day processes of the operations functions, such as front- and back-office functions, technology, performance improvement, management reporting and people management, then we must accept that each has a component of operational risk management embedded in it.

Operations management can therefore be a very real source and cause of the risk!

4

Managing the risk

How does the business manage operations risk?

The respective roles within the overall operational risk management process are vital. In my experience without clear reporting, communication and responsibility lines there is a significant possibility that risk events will be identified but not acted on in time or worse will fail to be identified at all.

In the previous chapter, we identified that there are three risks – standard, key and killer. The questions are to what extent does the management of each of the risks alter because of the profile of the risk, and to what extent is risk managed on a specific basis rather than or as well as collectively?

Operational risk management (ORM) requires a structure that will be credible, effective and cost efficient for the business. We may have made this point before but it is vitally important because the way in which ORM is perceived within a business is fundamental to how effective it will be.

Operations team's understanding of risk will vary. It is possible but not certain that a team dealing with derivatives may have more awareness and appreciation of risk given the characteristic of the product. Auditors and accountants may spend more time in carrying out their functions and tasks when dealing with derivatives because of the complexity of some types of derivatives. But, is the understanding and awareness risk associated with the product or the processes?

Fundamentally, operational risks are risks arising out of processes. Therefore, the basic ORM strategy must be geared towards identifying the critical process and the killer, key and standard risks associated with those processes. The processes may be manual or automated, continuous, frequent or periodic, relate to products, communication, systems or people.

Processes may involve decisions, instructions, payments, transference, data, services, be internal or externally related, or both. They can be integral to the actual business of an organisation, for instance invoicing and payments, or provide support for the business, for example management information or customer services.

It is not difficult to see that the types of risks associated with these processes will be varied and their impact equally varied. So, what is the risk management policy?

Devising a strategy to manage operations risk

The key questions must be:

- What is the strategy designed to achieve?
- What should it focus on?
- How can it be measured and monitored?
- Who is responsible for managing the risk?

In the bigger enterprise-wide risk management process we would consider analysing risk on a "bottom-up" or "top-down" basis. Is this appropriate in the operations risk environment?

Process-driven risks are created by a series of possibilities:

- Inadequacy of the process in the context of what it is supposed to achieve
- Lack of expertise in the people actioning the process
- Inadequacy of the technology supporting the process
- Poor management of the process
- Failure to alter the process to meet change.

Self-assessment techniques

Self-assessment of risk is vital, for as mentioned already it is the business and its people who are best placed to identify and manage risk, not risk managers. In operations the boys and girls in the front-line processes are, whether they realise it or not, dealing with risk on a day-to-day basis. Their supervisors and managers have the expertise relevant to the operations function in terms of product, structure, industry standards and operational management. They will also have knowledge of the historical issues and problems that have arisen.

This is vital input to any risk management process and it would be foolish in the extreme for it to be ignored. In fact, it must be the centre of the whole operations risk management process alongside which other risk views and measurement techniques can operate. No model can ever be more accurate than practical experience, no statistics as relevant as the "gut" feel of the experienced person. Within and without Barings there were many, many people who "sensed" something was wrong long before the actions of Leeson ever manifested themselves.

In some aspects of operational risk, the quantitative risk measurement process is both possible and desirable, with operations risk the subjective measurement processes will be far more beneficial and successful.

Does that mean no statistical analysis has merit and that no modelling is effective? No, far from it. Statistical data on errors is vital in the overall risk management process and any manager will make use of and act on the information on error source, frequency and impact because the reduction in errors is, or should be, a key objective of the operations manager.

Furthermore, the data on errors can be modelled to show any patterns that might be occurring and which might show an underlying problem. As this may relate to any one or more of the following table, the importance of analysing the available data on errors is obvious.

Risk envelope example

Risk envelopes	Type of risk	Price incorrect
Client statements	Incorrect value	Wrong settlement Client complaint
Profit/loss	Wrong calculation	Over/understated performance
Funding	Incorrect funding	Excess/shortfall in cash flow
Reporting	Exposure incorrect	Regulatory breach Risk data incorrect
Decisions	Under/overvalued input	Strategy outcome incorrect
Reputation	Published data wrong	Loss of business Regulatory issues

In the above example, the error of incorrect pricing has caused widespread potential errors across different aspects of the business and therefore increased the possibility of risk events occurring.

Operations risk management can also be illustrated as shown in Figure 4.1.

This combination provides for multiple risk profiles of the risk in the operations function to be established. This is important because the risk profiles may not always tell the same story.

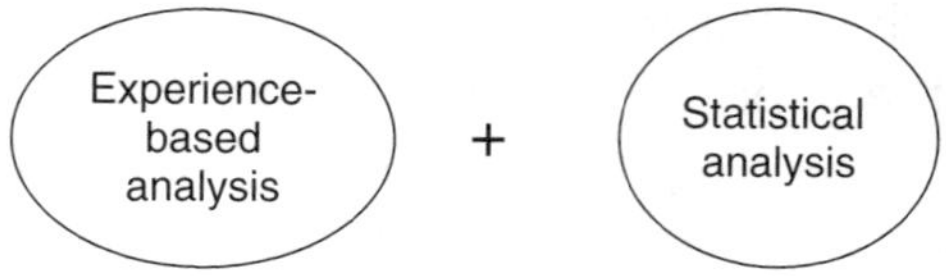

Figure 4.1 Extent of Risks Created by an Event

Example

Statistics may suggest that the level of errors in pricing a specific derivative position in the portfolio is too high. The experienced analysis of the operations manager/supervisor may suggest that the errors have insignificant impact and result from timing and source of price issues.

We need to be careful in our overall assessment of these two profiles.

First, if the statistics tell us that there is a level of errors that, in the context of the pricing benchmark, is high we need to analyse this further to establish if the benchmark, in relation to this product, is realistic.

Secondly, if the manager's experienced view is that the errors have insignificant impact, can some independent process of analysis confirm this?

Thirdly, the assertion that timing and price source are a contributory factor means we need to understand how material this is in terms of procedures and policy. For instance, on what basis was the product authorised for use if there were doubts about the timing and source of price information for valuation purposes?

The ability to realistically assess the type, level and impact of a risk that could occur in the operations universe is, as we have already established, vital. Let us therefore consider the types of risk measurement tools we have already mentioned, and debate further their advantages and disadvantages as well as look at other assessment techniques.

"Risk envelopes"

With this process, we look at identifying a series of "risk envelopes" and then seek to identify specific risk events that could happen and "map" these across the envelopes. The purpose is to ascertain where a risk event will manifest itself, how widespread the risk becomes if the event occurs and does it fall into a similar risk pattern compared to other risk events.

So is it effective?

Case study 1

Errors were being identified through the reconciliation process as being too frequent and potentially of a serious nature. However the reasons for the errors were not clear, but seemed to be related to trade input.

Through the self-assessment process the trade processing team had highlighted the volume of activity and problems with the trade input process from dealing system to back office system as being potential sources of risk.

The front office self-assessment process had also highlighted inconsistencies in the interface process as being a source of errors needing correction.

The overall impact of the two sources of problem was a risk event happening in the reconciliation process, that is the positions between the dealer record and operations system could not be agreed.

By mapping the risk resulting from the two self-assessments, the operational risk manager could see that the origins of the problem lay in the trade capture system, that it was impacting on trade input and was therefore ultimately arising as a risk event in the reconciliation process.

"Risk waves"

Risk waves are designed to enable the risk associated with a specific project or situation to be analysed in terms of the levels of actual against expected risk.

The main benefit here is the ability to measure the outcome of a project or situation and whether at the commencement of that project or situation the understanding of the risks and the impact of any delay or alteration were understood, anticipated or factored into the decisions and actions taken.

The technology and operations teams had reached a decision that a major enhancement to the operations trade processing and client service systems would be introduced through July and August and through December. The period from September to November was for assessment and adjustment in the live environment. The rationale was that activity levels would be at their lowest during these periods and the 3-month period of live operation would allow for "fine tuning" to take place.

Based on their rationale, the projected time for the full implementation of the enhancements was put at 6 months.

At the same time, the operations and technology managers had self-assessed the risk implications and had notified the operational risk managers that the potential for a risk event to happen would be increased during this implementation period. The probability of a risk event occurring was put at 25 per cent higher than average. The risk managers adjusted the operations function risk waves accordingly.

The first stage of the implementation was scheduled for the first weekend in July, however in June a final assessment by operations teams highlighted a series of minor changes that were needed.

Case study 2

The risk wave analysis shown above illustrates a number of risk scenarios together with their expected duration and level. If we take the case study above and then look at the risk wave profiles in Figure 4.2 we would have been initially looking at line A. This would show that the level of risk would rise substantially whilst the project is implemented followed by a sustained and significant fall in the risk level as the project is delivered, and finally a reduction in the target risk level as the full benefits of the implementation are realised.

The impact of the late request for changes will now be monitored.

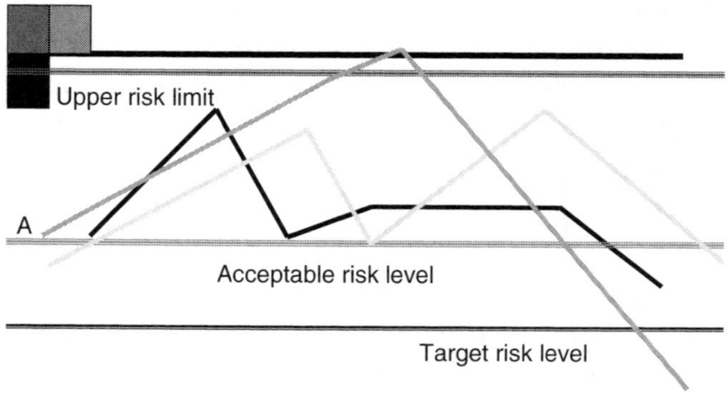

Figure 4.2 Utilising Risk Waves

Line A may steepen sharply and may also extend, in other words the level of risk increases above that expected and the duration of the increased risk level also increases.

The extent of this changed pattern needs to be carefully tracked.

Does the effect of the changes to the risk profile alter the level of procedures/controls that need to be in place?

Should additional capital be set aside if the probability of a risk event occurring has increased?

To what extent will any delay to the project impact across the business, that is what is the systemic risk within operations and outside of the operations function?

The risk wave analysis enables both the operations managers and the risk managers to be in control of the situation by providing a clear picture of how the project is progressing (in risk terms) and if the expected risk levels have been accurately assessed.

If there is no change to controls and procedures and the risk wave fundamentally deviates then the project risk is out of control; the operations and project managers are at fault and the risk manager must act!

"Risk scoring"

This measurement tool uses a series of scores based on frequency, impact and risk mitigation assessments. By assessing the risk and the risk mitigation we can get a better picture of actual risk. There is nothing new or scientific about the basic concept of scoring, indeed it is potentially highly subjective and the risk purists who seek mathematical quantative methods of measuring risks would be dismissive of risk scoring. On the other hand, operations managers, I know, will tell you that it is one of the most effective ways of measuring operations risk.

Risk scoring works on the basis of:

- Probability of the risk event happening
- Severity of the impact
- Quality of Preventative Controls.

The sum total indicates the level of risk and in addition can be compared to other risk evaluations under the risk-scoring process.

This has important connotations for the prioritisation of developments and projects to manage risk within operations.

There may be arguments for and against risk scoring, but the process of analysing the workflow, possible risk sources, impact and how the risk is being mitigated against can have tremendous spin offs in terms

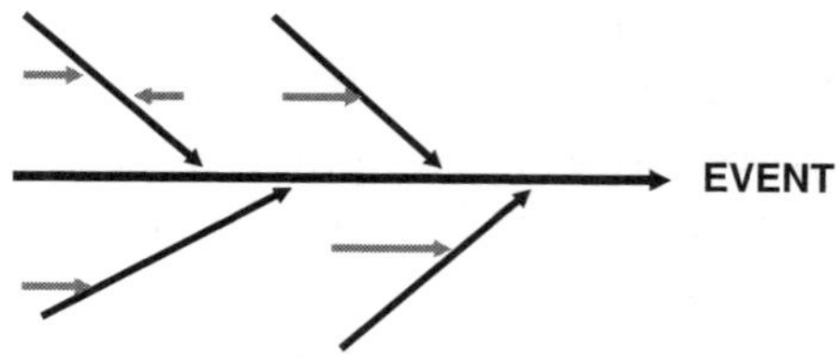

Figure 4.3 "Fishbone" Analysis of Cause

of resource planning, prioritisation of projects, staff training and development and business management such as budgeting.

Coming back to risk management, what else is there apart from risk scoring, risk waves and risk envelopes?

"Fishbone analysis of cause"

The "fishbone" analysis method seeks to track what is contributing, how, when and where to a risk event (Figure 4.3). It is particularly suited to the operations environment where typically an event is likely to have its root origins in processes within which a contributory factor could have occurred. Naturally the complexity of the process is a factor and makes the fishbone analysis even more relevant.

Case study: Risk incident with a corporate action

I have adapted this case study using an example of a fishbone analysis given in Christopher Marshall's excellent book *Measuring and Managing Operational Risks in Financial Markets*, published by Wiley.

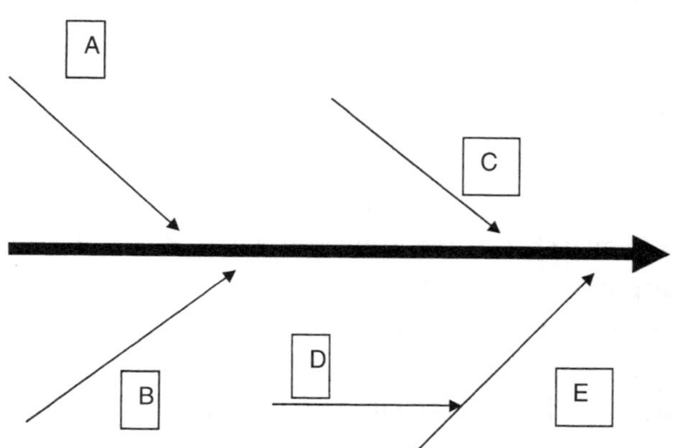

A – The initial instruction from a client regarding a corporate action, in this case a rights issue, is to "take no action".

B – Operations send instruction to custodian to that effect.

C – Custodian confirms to operations that the decision is "no action" although share price is rising.

D – Client sends second instruction to firm to now "take up rights". Operations send instruction to custodian.

Custodian seeks clarification of the instruction.

Another operations person looks for instruction details and finds original instruction – confirms to custodian "no action".

As a result the client's rights were allowed to lapse and the monetary value credited to the account. Later the client queries why the new shares have not been added to the position.

The firm has to buy shares in the market at a price now some 50% higher because the rights issue was a "success".

The error arose from series of incidents that started with a lack of control over the high risk process of instruction and instruction confirmations and then became compounded by a lack of awareness of the market so that the custodian's observation that the share price was moving, and the rights issue becoming therefore more attractive, was ignored.

Risk volcanoes

The risk volcano technique is one that assesses the possibility of a risk or a series of risk events happening that would create a situation where, if unchecked, the ultimate disaster could materialise (Figure 4.4).

If we assume that a volcano that erupts does so because of increasing pressure that finally is too much for the infrastructure of the volcanic mountain to contain, then we can apply this to a scenario that could exist within an operational environment. The centre of the pressure may well be within the operations environment or, alternatively, it may be the operations function that is consumed by such a massive disaster situation.

So what does the volcano involve?

It is in essence a cross between stress testing, scenario analysis and probability scoring mixed in with an assumption that mitigating controls fail on a systemic basis. In simple terms, it is analysing the risk environment in the operations structure to establish where weakness in controls, infrastructure, skills, resource, management, technology or processes may exist and where a combination of situations of failure could be catastrophic.

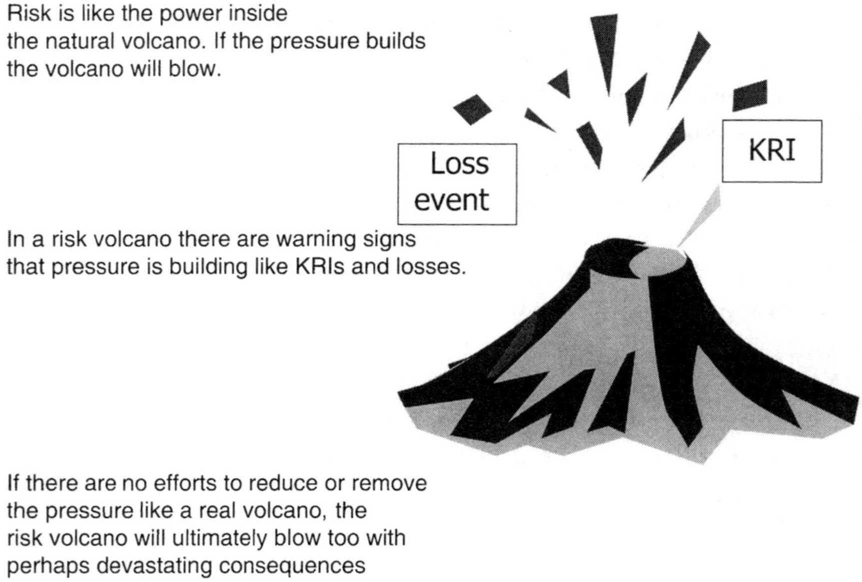

Figure 4.4 The Risk Volcano

Just like a real volcano, the chance of a "risk" volcano erupting totally unexpectedly and without any warning is remote. We can liken the activity within the actual volcano to the pressure building in an operations function, putting stress on procedures and processes and testing the controls mechanism.

As that pressure rises so the danger is increasing and with a real volcano we would begin to have evidence of this as maybe steam and smoke start to be emitted from the volcano. With our risk volcano what is the parallel?

We would expect to see the Key Risk Indicators (KRIs) showing increasing levels of "near misses". We would see actual losses occurring, similar to the actual volcano beginning to spew out lava. As the pressure rises the structure at the top of the volcano would begin to fail creating more and more evidence of an imminent eruption. In our risk volcano a similar scenario would be occurring as controls begin to fail to cope with the problems and the events become losses on an ever-increasing scale until a point of no return is reached and the business can no longer withstand what is happening.

The risk is out of control and a catastrophic consequence will be the outcome.

When this pressure cannot be controlled in the real volcano, the point of no return creates the awesome eruption that can be so powerful that much of the volcanic mountain ceases to exist. With our risk volcano the outcome can indeed be the same as Barings Bank was to find out.

An operations manager who is also managing the risk in the function must be able to analyse what combination of risk situations, failures, inadequacies and so on could occur and whether the controls will totally fail before the risk is realised, in other words "what is my risk volcano?"

Then the risk needs managing out!

Summary

There are many possible tools that can be used to manage operations risk and we will look later in the book at what might constitute an "operations risk management tool kit", however let us now look at the structure of a risk event.

5

Understanding a risk event

Risk events need defining, not least because, to paraphrase, one man's risk event is another's opportunity!

I am not being sarcastic when I say that too many risk managers and operations managers do not understand a risk event and certainly do not understand the anatomy of a risk event.

So what is a "risk event"?

What constitutes a risk event depends on the business. In the air traffic control business, a "near miss" is a risk event. In banking, a fraud is a risk event.

Risk events are essentially a situation that creates a financial or reputation loss as far as the business is concerned. Elsewhere in the book we have already ascertained that the risk event may be a routine risk, a key risk or, in extreme cases, a killer risk.

Figure 5.1 illustrates the anatomy of a risk event.

We see a very structured situation simply because risk events are, in virtually all cases, very structured.

Four principal stages happen in all risk events.

1. Pre-event
2. Time Lag
3. Realisation
4. Mitigation.

Pre-event

In the pre-event stage we are hoping that the risk awareness of the people, the effectiveness of the controls, and so on will be sufficient that

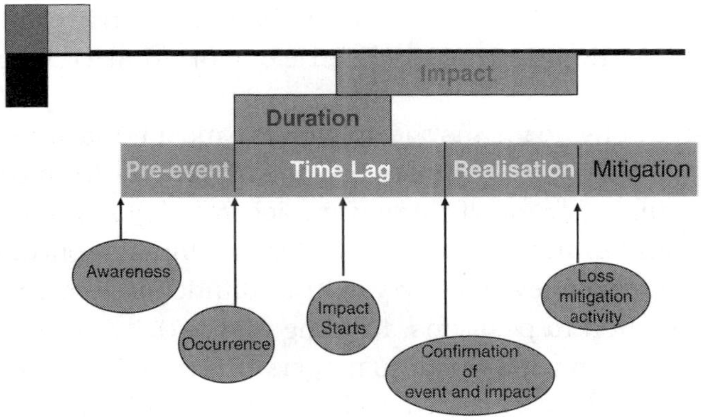

Figure 5.1 Understanding a Risk Event

the risk event is managed before it materialises into a full-blown risk event, that is a loss has actually happened. The period that constitutes the "pre-event" can be quite short or in some cases prolonged, running into weeks, months and in some cases even years.

When a risk event happens the operations manager will want to analyse what occurred in the pre-event stage. Did the controls fail? Were they ignored? Was the event not predicted?

The pre-event stage is when the extent of success of the risk awareness training will be evident. The better the culture the more risk events are captured at the pre-event stage. We will look at developing the risk culture in a later chapter, however from the operations manager's point of view it will be disappointing if there are many risk events actually happening. If there are it will be partly because there is a problem with identifying the risk event. The key to the extent that the risk event becomes a major incident can usually be directly linked to the time lag before it is actually realised that the event is happening. It stands to reason that if a firm is not aware that a risk event is happening the possibility of significant loss is highly likely.

Case study – Barings Bank

One of the reasons that the Bank collapsed was undoubtedly the apparent lack of awareness that several key controls were failing and that a very significant financial loss was happening. The collapse of Barings has been well documented and the reader should refer to the list of suggested reading in the appendices if they are not familiar with the full details of what happened, however we will consider here the operations-related elements that contributed to the collapse.

The first, but by no means the only, or the most important contributor was the failure to segregate the role of a trader from that of an operations manager, or, if there were acceptable logistical reasons for Leeson undertaking both roles, a clearly defined reporting structure and increased levels of oversight and independent verification of reports related to positions, funding and activity. This situation seemingly went on with senior managers unaware that a major risk environment had been created and that as a result risk events were not only quite likely, they were in fact already occurring.

The second operations risk issue concerned the reconciliation process. Leesons trading activity initially was for the London and Tokyo trading books. He was an order filler rather than a trader, meaning that he completed trades rather than taking trading decisions himself. The trades he carried out on the then called SIMEX exchange in Singapore were of course reported back by him to London and were reconciled to the trade details that the London and Tokyo traders reported. This process was sound and was not the cause of the problem that ultimately destroyed the bank.

However, Leeson began to trade on the now infamous "88888" or error account where he posted loss-making trades. In the context of risk an error account must be very closely monitored and a reconciliation process must happen to ensure (a) that all errors are recorded and (b) that they have been properly represented in the Profit and Loss account. At Barings, the 88888 account was not independently reconciled nor was its losses included in the Profit and Loss account.

A third and equally important failure was the inability to recognise the very significant risk that the funding of Leeson's activities was creating, a risk that could only be justified if the apparent return on capital employed, that is his reported profits could unequivocally be proven. The level of funding for derivatives trades, mainly futures and some options could only have been for either massive open positions or massive losses. The funding could not have been proven for the return on capital because the error account was being excluded, nor could it have been funding for massive positions because the internal records showed the trading books within their limits and so a "black hole" amounting to hundreds of millions of pounds sterling was in existence but nobody was seemingly aware of it.

> The last operations related situation I want to highlight here concerns culture. In Singapore it would not have been likely that a more junior person would have questioned Leeson's actions whilst in say London or New York, whilst not certain, it would have been more probable that his actions in hiding the loss-making trades in the error account would have been escalated to senior managers.

Time lag

The time taken to realise that the risk event has happened can be crucial for a number of reasons.

First, no organisation or operations area is so perfect in its risk management process that a risk event will never occur. What matters in terms of the effectiveness of the risk management process is the speed with which an event, if it happens, is discovered by the control processes the operations manager employs. A long time lag may be an indication of poor monitoring or may be a natural result of the risk event being obscured by something else. An important factor in minimising the likely time lag before an event being realised is the quality of the Key risk indicators (KRIs) and Key performance indicators (KPIs). These measures are explained more fully later in the chapter and elsewhere in the book.

The time lag is also influenced by the robustness of the self-assessment techniques of the operations teams and supervisors. This illustrates, perhaps, the importance that must be attached to the self-assessment process in being a source of identifying possible risk events. The more robust the process is the better the control over events will be, including rapid identifying of an event happening.

Realisation

The phase of realisation can be one of panic or organised chaos! In reality of course a cool head, clear procedures and a positive approach to the risk event is what is needed not headless chickens and blame apportioning, neither of which are of any use whatsoever.

The event having occurred needs mitigation but before that can be fully introduced the profile of the event needs to be established and quickly.

The template for assessing the risk event occurrence would look something like this for the first stage.

Event type	Unknown	Standard	Key	Killer
Inception	Unknown	Estimated date	Unverified date	Verified date
Impact location(s)				
Origin location(s)				
Risk envelopes				
Control point	Supervisor	Manager	Senior manager	Risk manager
Escalation	Manager	Senior manager	Risk manager	Board
Incident report	Prepared	Checked	Distributed	Affirmed
Remedial action	Yes	No	Not certain	
Second stage activated	Yes	No	Not certain	

Also, at realisation is the key issue of "escalation".

Clear procedures on what to do once the risk event is discovered might look like this:

- List of supervisors and managers for initial reporting
- Compilation of an initial risk event report
- Operational Risk Officer (ORO) for Manager/Department(s) with ownership advised
- Mitigation team provide initial response(s)
- Rectifying Actions authorised by department/manager
- ORO reports to Risk Management Group
- Manager/Department provide detailed Incident Report
- Incident Database (including if appropriate Loss Database) updated
- Details on incident circulated to OROs for "lessons learned" exercise
- Risk Group/Business advised on suggested amendments/ enhancements to risk management procedures
- Risk Group/Business sign off on Event.

Mitigation

Once an event is occurring and is realised there must be action taken to mitigate the impact. Naturally, this should be instigated as quickly as possible but it is essential that the action taken is both practical and effective.

The business unit itself is usually by far the best people to deal with the result of the event, never forget it is their business not the risk group's. The risk group and in particular the OROs (or their equivalent) can offer advice and through the procedures outlined above will be involved in monitoring the progress towards successful closing of the event.

It is important to understand that there are lessons to be learned from all and any event, and those lessons when mapped onto other business units may highlight an enhancement to procedures and controls, which might prevent a similar event happening in that business unit.

Lessons learned

It is important therefore that the OROs not only monitor but also review and assess the data on the event and apply their judgements in the context of lessons learned. This is another illustration of where real added value for the business as a whole can be achieved.

What would the ORO look for?

The following is an illustration of the contents of an Event Lessons Learned Checklist:

1. Time to realisation?
2. Was the event covered in the self-assessment of the area?
3. Was the assessment correct at the time?
4. Had the event previously registered as a "near miss"?
5. Did KRIs/KPIs work?
6. If no – why?
7. If yes – why did the information not get acted on?
8. Did preventative controls fail to identify the potential event?
9. Was the time lag from inception too impact to short for preventative controls to work?
10. Were preventative controls ignored?
11. Did preventative controls only partially work and if so why?
12. Which type of process/situation in the unit is similar?
13. Is the risk event common to other processes/situations?
14. Do other business units have similar processes/situations?
15. What other observations on lessons to be learned are there?

OROs analysis should then be compiled and distributed to the Risk Manager and other OROs so that the lessons learned can be discussed with the business.

Remember that the whole purpose of active operations risk management is not to point the finger or to apportion blame but simply:

1. To ensure that the event is understood
2. Its impact has been terminated and
3. Any lessons have been learnt.

6

Workflow and operations risk

The workflow within an organisation is a major source of operations risk. This comes about because of the significant involvement of

1. People
2. Processes
3. Technology.

There are other participants and influences, such as third parties, activity levels, etc, but we will focus on the "big" three and comment on the others as they arise.

People

Wherever there is human intervention or participation in any process there is a risk of error and/or poor performance together with a possibility of deliberate criminal act, malicious action and incompetence that could also be negligent.

The operations risk that any particular organisation faces is primarily linked to the business activity, structure, management and risk appetite.

When considering the sources of risk, as these are major influences, it stands to reason that it is important to be in a position to fully understand the nature of the business itself. Added to this is the requirement to fully recognise and understand the role and involvement of various parts of the operations function in the business of the firm.

For instance, a customer-facing unit such as a help-desk facility has not only a crucial role to play in the success of the business but is

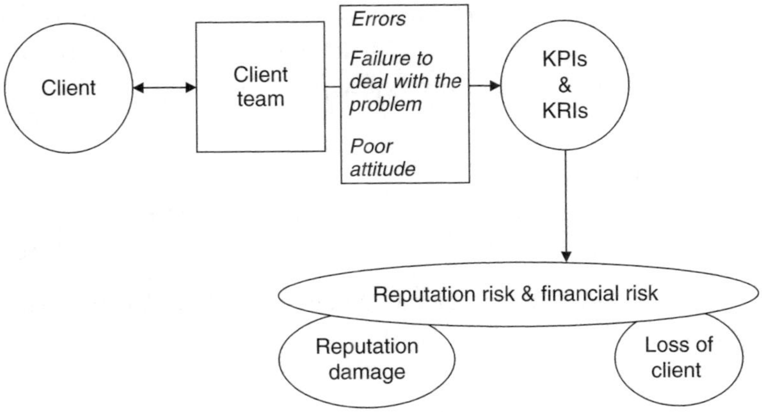

Figure 6.1 Root Causes

also a massive source of potential risk events and potential reputation damage (Figure 6.4).

Most people would realise this is the case but realising and being risk-aware are not necessarily the same thing.

What for instance is going to tell us that there is a problem? We would expect that the KPIs at least would show a deterioration in the service levels but be careful as that is not always the case.

Root causes as shown above are undoubtedly identifiable and manageable. Management information, complaint logs, and so on should be providing the data to the KPIs and KRIs that would indicate that there were problems with the service delivery from the Client Team.

Monitoring of client activity will provide additional evidence of any tail off in business, although this may of course have nothing to do with the performance of the client team and could be caused by, for instance, a change of personnel or business profile at the client's.

It is also worth mentioning here that the client's perception of the service they receive is not necessarily consistent with the actual service level delivered. It is important that this is addressed but the ability to control the level of risk is dependent on the level of client relationship that can be maintained. It is inevitable that in firms with large client bases the level of attention paid to a small client is probably not going to be the same as that given to the bigger value client. The possibility of picking up that there is a potential problem is therefore restricted to either the client making a formal complaint (may not happen and could be too late to rescue) or to being able to identify the situation via data (may not show anything as it is the client's perception).

So the impact of the people on operations risk may not always be clear cut. However, there are situations where the people impact is very obvious. For instance, we can look at an example of where the resolution of client enquiries is neither speedy nor satisfactory in outcome. The causes could be many. These are a few possibilities:

- Poorly trained personnel
- Lack of motivation
- Ineffective management and leadership of the team
- Inadequate source of information to be able to provide solutions.

If we take these separately we can follow a likely path to a risk event (see fishbone analysis in Chapter 4).

Poorly trained personnel

Dealing with clients and relationship skills are a fairly specialist's skills set. Individuals need to have personality, a good level of communication skills, knowledge of the services being offered, knowledge of the client's business and use of those services, be organised and be able to see tasks through to completion.

Lack of motivation

This can be caused by various factors and combination of factors. Poor management in terms of guidance and support for staff, leaving them feeling exposed to problems could be one. A poor quality product or service creating continuous complaints and little possibility of a satisfactory resolution would be another.

Under-resourcing and non-recognition of the importance of the role by management and colleagues can be highly demotivating.

Management

It is a fact that management is a source of operations risk. The classic reason is over promotion, that is the individual does not possess the skills to carry out the role and yet is given the position. This can happen for a number of reasons but is likely to be either a "reward" for long-standing loyalty to the company (today this is less common) or happens because of poor management decisions elsewhere.

Today, a much more valid reason for management being a source of operations risk is the sheer pressure on the person and their team.

Most managers are under severe stress. They may not admit it, some may actually enjoy it and perform well because of it, but for many firms it is a (semi) hidden but critical source of risk. Why senior management seems quite often oblivious to it is a bit of a mystery. I am not aware that any major business school advocates putting managers under stress as a key element of successful business management. The possible financial and reputational loss to the firm concerned will in all probability be significant and certainly talent will be submerged and then destroyed by the pressure.

Nevertheless, most managers are operating with high levels of pressure, much of it unnecessary and as a consequence the overall risk level of the firm is high when it need not be.

Analysing risk in the workflow

Managers and supervisors must understand the risks in the workflow they are responsible for.

One obvious question that this poses is how to analyse the risk in an objective and practical way?

The workflow itself may present some interesting angles on how to approach the analysis. For instance, a heavily manual process can present greater risk possibilities whilst in theory a heavily automated process reduces the potential risks. This is a simplistic view and may in reality have little basis. Many manual processes can possess few risks. Many automated processes contain high levels of risk. Assumption is a "killer risk" and very often the mistake is made in treating manual processes as risky and automated processes as risk-free.

So what are we analysing?

Workflow consists of processes and process is a source of risk. The workflow processes can consist amongst others:

- Continuous processes
- Intermittent processes
- Processes on demand
- Cyclical processes
- Client-driven processes.

We need to ascertain whether there are particular key or even killer risks associated in the processes undertaken in the section. In this context the key risks may be:

- Process reliability
- Operatives knowledge/understanding/competence
- Critical deadlines
- Dependency
- Process relevance
- Influences on the process.

If we look at each of these we can see how the importance is established and why the analysis is relevant.

Process reliability

The objectives and outcome of any process must be a critical factor in why the process is being carried out at all. The reliability of the process is therefore essential or otherwise why is it being done? If the process is for instance a reconciliation then the objectives are on the face of it obvious. It must be reliable in its outcome, that is, it must provide certainty of fact – the position is agreed for example. If the outcome of the process is in doubt then there is a degree of risk, possibly a high degree of risk.

So we have to analyse the probability of the process not being performed or being performed incorrectly or being performed late.

Key to this will be:

- Frequency of non-performance
- Incidents of incorrect process
- Frequency of late performing of the process.

Then we need to analyse the probable impact of any of these situations. Once we have these factors we can determine whether we have a possible key or killer risk situation.

Analysing workflow

All operations managers analyse workflow and therefore they will have an idea of the stress points, weaknesses, variables, and so on.

Analysing the workflow from a risk-specific point of view will add value to the normal workflow analysis and provide for greater efficiencies and performance.

What is risk-specific analysis?

This, like much of operations risk, is business-related and as we have said before a complex process and/or product will produce a different profile to a high volume but basic process and/or product.

Figure 6.2 shows a very generic, workflow analysis.

The workflow associated with a specific product will obviously also carry the operations risks. Figures 6.3 and 6.4 illustrate the process for two derivative products, in this case an over-the-counter option and a credit default swap.

These road maps show the process for these products and the key stages in the road map are also key areas in terms of potential operations risk.

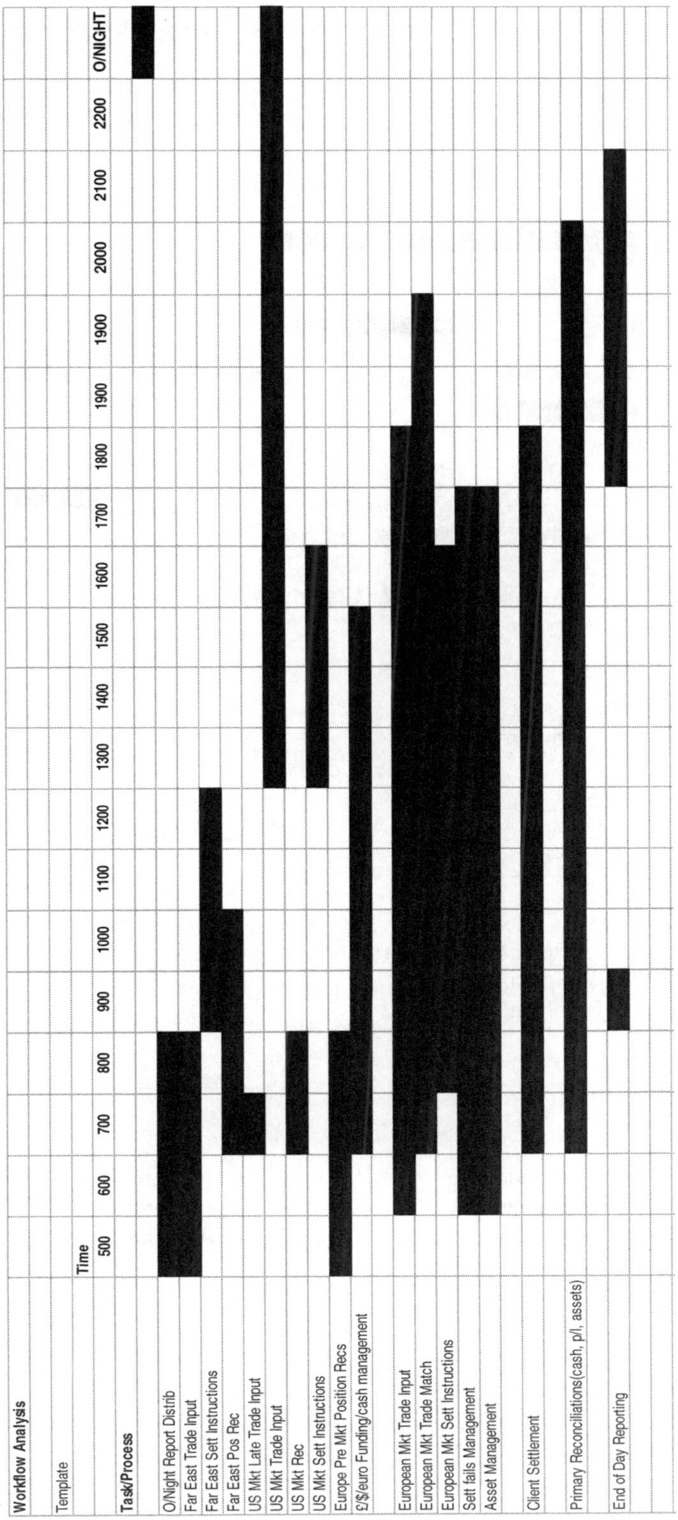

Figure 6.2 Workflow Analysis

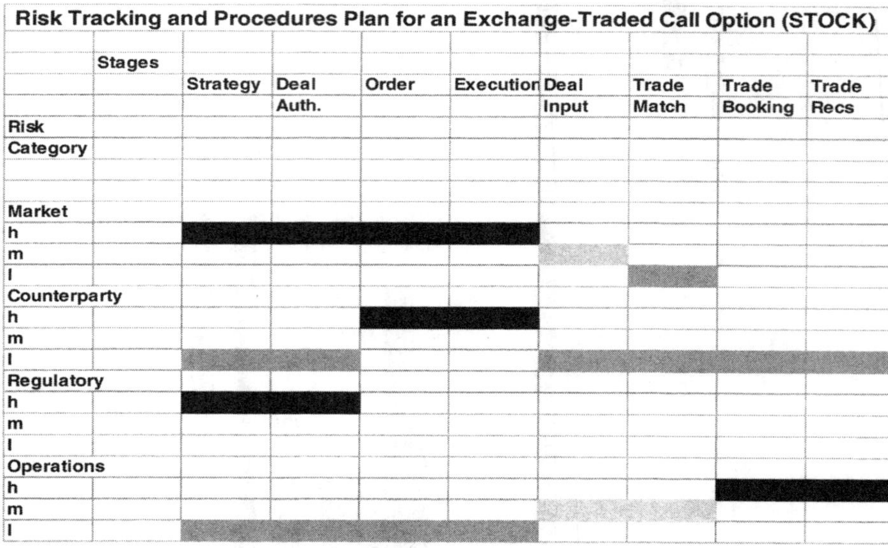

Figure 6.2 (*Continued*)

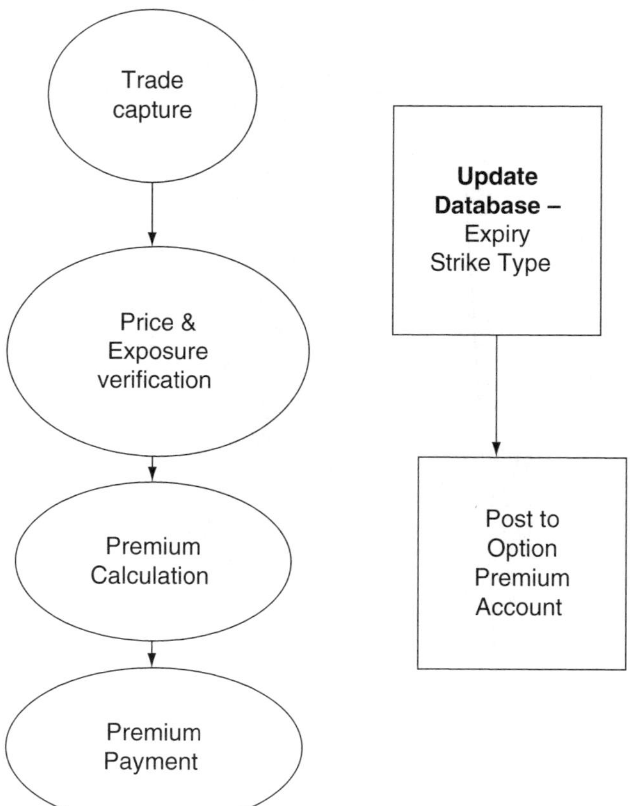

Figure 6.3 OTC Option road map

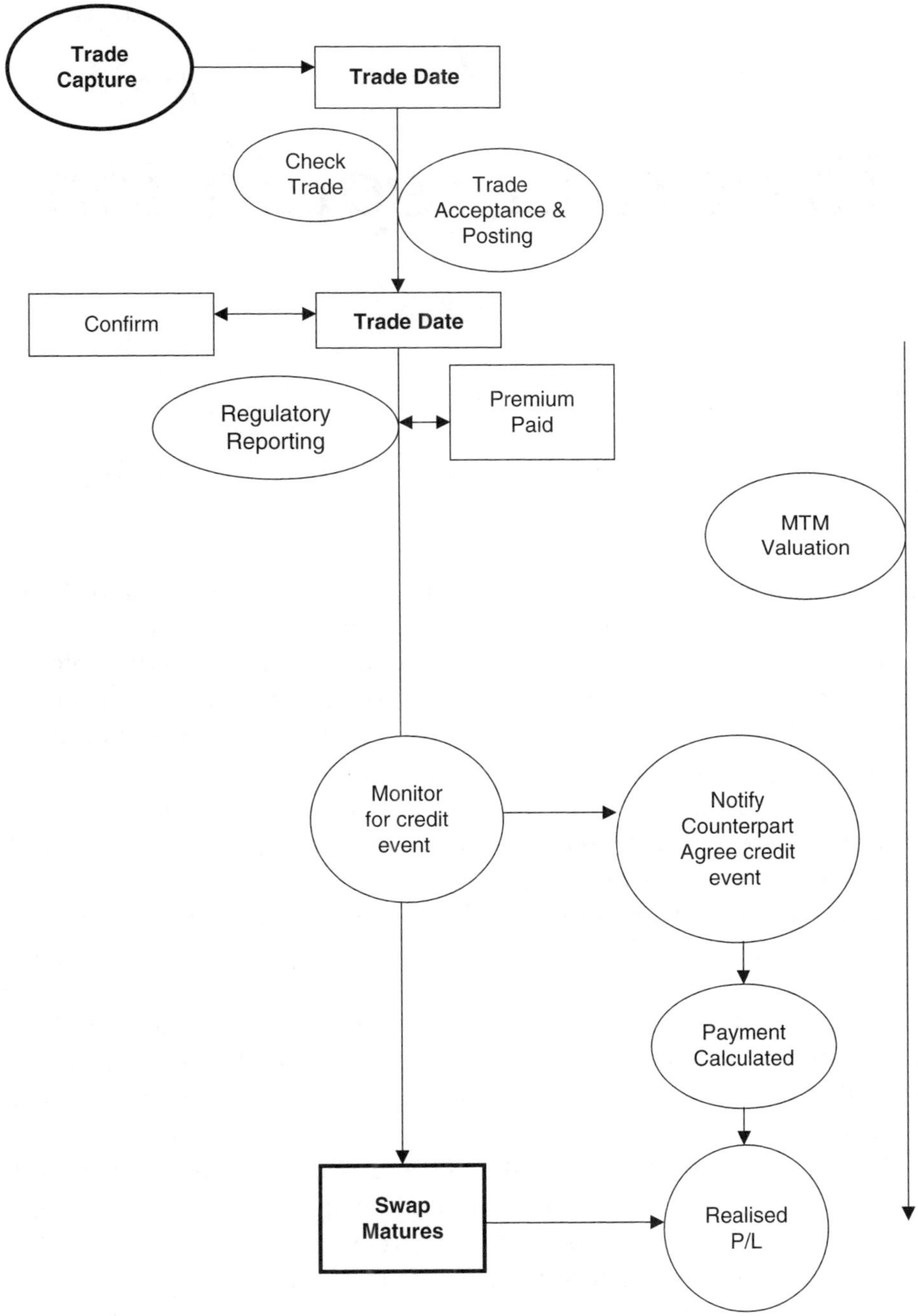

Figure 6.4 Road map for a Credit Default Swap transaction

7

Risk and regulation

It is difficult and, indeed for completeness, somewhat essential that the question of the regulation of risk should at least be explored.

It is not intended to go into great detail about the regulation related to operational and operations risk, that is covered very well in many other publications, but it is important to identify what regulation does have an impact in terms of the operations teams.

Most focus tends to be on the revised Basel Accord, known as Basel II, but there are other regulations that carry elements of operational risk requirement. For instance, the Sarbanes–Oxley Act in the United States, the Markets in Financial Instruments Directive (MiFID) and UCITs III Directive in Europe all create requirements for operational risk management.

Each regulatory jurisdiction also has its own regulation that applies, for example that of the Financial Services Authority (FSA) in the United Kingdom or the Securities and Exchange Commission in the United States.

The FSA have Conduct for Business (COB) Rules that require amongst other things a firm to deal with its customers in a professional way and to protect their assets under the relevant section of the Rules called Customer Assets (CASS). This is where the issues about segregation of client money and assets from that of the firm affect the operations teams.

The Bank for International Settlement (BIS) published Sound Practices for the Management and Supervision of Operational Risk in February 2003 and any operations manager should have read this and ideally had their supervisors and team leaders read it as well.

In the Introduction to the document the BIS states:

Introduction

1. The following paper outlines a set of principles that provide a framework for the effective management and supervision of operational risk for use by banks and supervisory authorities when evaluating operational risk management policies and practices.
2. The Basel Committee on Banking Supervision (the Committee) recognises that the exact approach for operational risk management chosen by an individual bank will depend on a range of factors, including its size and sophistication and the nature and complexity of its activities. However, despite these differences, clear strategies and oversight by the board of directors and senior management, a strong operational risk culture and internal control culture (including, among other things, clear lines of responsibility and segregation of duties), effective internal reporting, and contingency planning are all crucial elements of an effective operational risk management framework for banks of any size and scope. The Committee therefore believes that the principles outlined in this paper establish sound practices relevant to all banks.

Source: BIS

The full document is available at the BIS website where it describes the suggested "Sound Practices" through a series of "Principles".

To give the reader an idea of this, an excerpt covering Principle 4 of 10 is given below.

Principle 4

Banks should identify and assess the operational risk inherent in all material products, activities, processes and systems. Banks should also ensure that before new products, activities, processes and systems are introduced or undertaken, the operational risk inherent in them is subject to adequate assessment procedures.

What, apart from client money and assets, are other areas of regulation that apply or are relevant in respect of operational risk and within its operations risk?

Regulation in respect of custody services

Custodians have only comparatively recently become the subject of specific regulatory oversight partially due to the recognition of the risks associated with the provisions of custody and safekeeping but also because of the increasingly more diversified and in some cases complex services being offered to clients.

Regulation affecting brokers and fund management companies

Other than the already-mentioned client assets and money rules there are also rules about taking on customers, dealing with complaints, marketing and sales and of course confidentiality of client data.

For example, the following is Principle 9 of the Conduct of Business Rules of the FSA.

> **Principle 9 (Customers: Relationships of trust)** requires a *firm* to take reasonable care to ensure the suitability of its advice and discretionary decisions. To comply with this, a *firm* should obtain sufficient information about its *private customer* to enable it to meet its responsibility to give suitable advice. A *firm* acting as a discretionary *investment manager* for a *private customer* should also ensure that before acting in the exercise of discretion it has sufficient information about its *private customer* to enable it to act in a way which is suitable for that *private customer*.

Here is an example of the rules relating to client money and assets again from the FSA.

> **CASE 4.3.2**
>
> The purpose of the *client money rules* is to ensure that, unless otherwise permitted, *client money* is kept separate from the *firm's* own *money*. Segregation, in the event of a *firm's failure*, is important for the effective operation of the statutory trust that is created to protect *client money*. The aim is to clarify the difference between *client money* and general creditors' entitlements in the event of the *failure* of the *firm*.

Failure by the operations team to comply with these kinds of client-related regulatory requirements is going to be dealt, quite probably harshly, by the regulator. Controls and procedures to ensure compliance has occurred and are essential, and these must not only be included in the procedure manual of the firm but should be regularly reviewed for effectiveness by managers and supervisors.

Exchange and clearing house regulation

There are various regulations imposed on members by exchanges and clearing houses. These often relate to the operations areas such as reporting, confirmation and settlement. For example, in the exchange-traded derivatives market there are requirements imposed on clearing members relating to the settlement of their customers (if applicable) and their own obligations in futures and options traded on the relevant exchange. Failure to carry out this function by the required time can, in the most serious situation, result in the member being declared in "default" (which if it did not terminate the business it would severely damage it) or at the very least could lead to the withdrawal of the firm's membership. Either is obviously massively damaging in terms of reputation and also financial loss (fines, loss of clients, etc.).

There are also often regulations relating to the performance of systems, managers, and so on, related to being accepted as a member or maintaining an ongoing membership.

Summary details on regulation

As already noted, there is a lot of information on regulation and so there is in the appendices some further comment and information on this subject.

Regulatory risk is an operational risk and as a result it is important to understand the types of regulatory risks that a business faces.

Irrespective of the business, there are generic risks like:

- Breach of regulation applicable to a firm
- Client money breaches
- Client confidentiality breaches
- Money Laundering Regulation
- Failure to provide required reports to the regulator
- Late filing of reports.

Each of these usually involves processes and procedures that are being run and implemented by the operations team.

An ORO must be very aware of these issues especially with respect to their own particular business area.

Summary

It is extremely important to understand that in today's employment environment life style management issues can be a very major operational risk and a massive challenge for operations managers.

Employees that are placed under stressful situations may not only perform poorly and therefore affect risk but may be so affected that law suits may follow.

The laws affecting the workplace in terms of diversity and other personnel-related issues are not simply something for HR to worry about, they are very much in the operations managers' domain.

The manager needs to look out for the following situations and devise, together with HR, a suitable solution:

- Diversity training covering prejudice, sexism, ageism, etc.
- Peer pressures related to drinking, drugs, etc.
- Pressure to work long hours or anti-social hours
- Discrimination against employees who resist unreasonable demands in the workplace
- Failure to recognise pressure and stress affecting employees, i.e. not realising tell-tale signs like illness, etc.
- Creating, within the workplace structure and workflow, a process that delivers a positive and effective life style management for all levels of employees.

8

Innovative tools to manage people risks

We have seen how personnel risk is a key issue for organisations and we have noted that areas like loss of key personnel, difficult recruitment environments, and so on can have a major impact on risk levels, particularly in operations. However, today's business environment has created other types of risk associated with people like stress, confidence issues and motivational issues. Finding the appropriate tools to help manage these types of risk issues requires an open mind and vision to adopt "new" ways of addressing the problems.

One of my colleagues is Rachel Davis BA (Hons), D.Hyp, BSCH (Assoc.) Clinical Hypnotherapist and here she is able to give us a brief insight into just how effective some tools that enable solutions to lifestyle management and individual employee support challenges can be.

Analysing Hypnotherapy as a tool to reduce operations risk

It is important not to underestimate the part an individual can play in mitigating the effects of operational risk in a firm. In instances where an individual has underlying personal and work issues, which are not resolved, this can have a negative impact on their performance, which can also have wider implications for the firm.

Examples of these issues may include:

- Stress management
- Goal setting and time management
- Performance-related anxiety

Stress management

Some pressure is vital in fast-paced environments, and is in fact a healthy part of performance. However, work-related stress can be detrimental and often results when an individual feels out of control. An individual's focus is internalised and impinges on their ability to remain calm and objective in situations which can in turn create problems within their working environment, where deadlines are missed, mistakes are made and communications can suffer with a resulting breakdown in working relationships. Individuals need to have a workable stress plan in order to learn how to identify stress triggers and they can then start to develop strategies with which to change their negative reaction to stressful situations to a positive reaction. They also need to understand how to relax and start to take control of those situations which create their stress.

Goal setting and time management

Both the firm and its employees will have a range of identifiable goals, which may not be achieved within a prescribed timeframe. This can be demoralising not only for the individual, but can also have a negative impact on the organisation. Staff struggling to manage their time effectively can loose their motivation and feel under extreme pressure to meet deadlines resulting in a lack of attention to detail and a general feeling of malaise.

Individuals who learn techniques to manage their time effectively are more able to reach their goals, overcoming previously held perceived obstacles to success through changing any self-limiting beliefs and behaviours. From an operational risk perspective, effective timing is crucial and staff who are able to meet deadlines will feel motivated, which in turn will have a positive impact on the organisation.

Performance-related anxiety

It is natural to feel a sense of nervousness when individuals are in unfamiliar situations, such as making a presentation to an important client, delivering a key speech to a room full of people or even in everyday dealings with different departments within the firm. It can often be seen that these feelings can become all-consuming and inhibit an individual from performing at their best.

If individuals can develop a positive mental frame of mind, these natural feelings of anxiety can be channelled into feelings of excitement and energy, which can not only improve their performance but also enhance their interpersonal management skills.

Hypnotherapy

One of the tools available to individuals who want to work through these issues is Hypnotherapy. Hypnosis is a natural state of absorbed concentration combined with heightened awareness, which is a state experienced by individuals at various times throughout their everyday life when they are day dreaming, engrossed in a book, watching television or driving. Individuals are guided into the state of hypnosis by a hypnotherapist to work to change patterns of behaviour, which will therefore remove obstacles which prevent individuals from reaching their potential.

What happens in a hypnotherapy session?

There are various stages to a hypnotherapy session:

- Taking a case history. Discussion and agreeing the goal for therapy and providing a full explanation of hypnosis.
- Achieving the trance state – this can be achieved in a number of ways, however usually the individual sits in a semi-reclined position and listens to the hypnotherapist talking in a slow and soothing voice. They might be asked to imagine walking down a country lane or to listen to the sound of the therapist's voice and very often suggestions for relaxation are also given. The trance is deepened using a countdown from 10 to 1, the patient will feel very relaxed but completely aware of their surroundings.
- Awakening the patient – the therapist may count up from 1 to 10 to return the patient to full consciousness, but this can also be achieved by the patient themselves.
- The first session is usually approximately one-and-a-half hours in duration, with subsequent sessions of one hour.
- Some therapy may involve only one session, whilst others may require 5 to 6 sessions.

Working with a hypnotherapist on underlying personal and work issues can mitigate some of the factors which if left unresolved can create instances of operational risk in a firm. (More details about the services available in this field can be found at www.dscportfolio.com.)

The concept Rachel has outlined above is clearly not one that many managers or firms would perhaps consider or associate with risk management, and yet as the whole process of understanding risks and then finding solutions evolves it is precisely this type of somewhat radical approach that is defining the leaders in operational risk management.

In addition, the spin offs to an organisation from providing facilities for individuals to address issues they have of a personal nature is pretty self-evident and the correlation between performance and morale, pressure and risk is increasingly understood by risk, business and operations managers. It is also important to remember that whilst the use of say hypnotherapy is not directly about revenue or cost savings, it is a fact that the spin offs that lead to higher morale and performance can make the whole process highly cost-effective.

9

Insourcing and outsourcing risk

There has been a significant trend in the financial markets for some years to outsource various functions normally carried out by the firm itself. These functions can include but are not restricted to:

- Technology
- Client help desks and call centres
- Administration
- Pricing and valuations.

Of course, some functions have been outsourced for many years either because of regulation or choice, for example custody and safe-keeping.

The operational and operations risk that occurs in any insource/outsource situation can be very significant, a fact recognised by the BIS which published in August 2004 a consultative paper by The Joint Forum called **Outsourcing in Financial Services**. In the paper the Forum gave "Guiding Principles" on the outsourcing issue and they are reproduced below.

Guiding principles – Overview

The Joint Forum has developed the following high-level principles. The first seven principles cover the responsibilities of regulated entities when they outsource their activities, and the last two principles cover regulatory roles and responsibilities. Here we present an overview of the principles. More detail may be found in Section 9. (*Note*: The full document is available at the BIS website.)

I. A regulated entity seeking to outsource activities should have in place a comprehensive policy to guide the assessment of whether and how those activities can be appropriately outsourced. The board of directors or equivalent body retains responsibility for the outsourcing policy and related overall responsibility for activities undertaken under that policy.
II. The regulated entity should establish a comprehensive outsourcing risk management programme to address the outsourced activities and the relationship with the service provider.
III. The regulated entity should ensure that outsourcing arrangements neither diminish its ability to fulfil its obligations to customers and regulators nor impede effective supervision by regulators.
IV. The regulated entity should conduct appropriate due diligence in selecting third-party service providers.
V. Outsourcing relationships should be governed by written contracts that clearly describe all material aspects of the outsourcing arrangement, including the rights, responsibilities and expectations of all parties.
VI. The regulated entity and its service providers should establish and maintain contingency plans, including a plan for disaster recovery and periodic-testing of backup facilities.
VII. The regulated entity should take appropriate steps to require that service providers protect confidential information of both the regulated entity and its clients from intentional or inadvertent disclosure to unauthorised persons.
VIII. Regulators should take into account outsourcing activities as an integral part of their ongoing assessment of the regulated entity. Regulators should assure themselves by appropriate means that any outsourcing arrangements do not hamper the ability of a regulated entity to meet its regulatory requirements.
IX. Regulators should be aware of the potential risks posed where the outsourced activities of multiple regulated entities are concentrated within a limited number of service providers.

The reader is really encouraged to obtain the full document as clearly the operations risk in outsource/insource described in a high level above is very considerable. At the end of the document, in the Annex, are some examples of the problems experienced by very different organisations in an insource/outsource arrangement (see below). Whilst obviously not every arrangement will end up as the kind of problem experienced by these organisations, the possibility is clearly there.

Case study 1: German loan factory

In Germany, an increasing number of credit institutions outsource loan handling to specialised, unregulated service providers, called "loan factories". These service providers specialise in backoffice services concerning loans and mortgages, and in some cases deciding whether to grant a loan.

In 2003, a credit institution wanted to outsource not only the servicing of loans, but also the decision to grant a loan in standard retail-lending-business and in the non-standard-business up to € 2.5 million.

The result of the assessment by the supervisor was that in the non-standard-business the credit institution was unable to monitor and oversee the loans granted by the loan factory. Though the business is run by the credit institution, which bears the risk emerging from it, the decision on granting the loans had been made by the service provider.

Issues which emerged as part of this scenario included:

- The outsourcing of decisions concerning the incurrence of new exposure is permissible only if it does not impair the management's ability to manage risks adequately.
- The aforementioned would only be met if the regulated entity stringently committed the service provider to apply precise and verifiable evaluation and assessment criteria. With the systems currently used by the financial industry, this is only possible in the standardised retail lending business.

Case study 2: Australian regulator investigates bank outsourcing

Australian banks have outsourced activities including information technology, credit card services, procurement, cheque and other electronic clearing services, mortgage processing and payroll amongst others. This raises questions about the privacy of customer information, the financial and reputational risks to the banks if a service provider experiences problems or cannot go on providing.

In January 2002, the Australian Prudential Regulation Authority (APRA) completed a targeted review of bank outsourcing, and introduced detailed prudential standards from 1 July 2002.

APRA found that outsourcing arrangements were managed in a number of ways. Larger institutions generally had a dedicated outsourcing unit responsible for ensuring that the institution's outsourcing policy is applied consistently. However, a number of institutions delegated responsibility for outsourcing to business units. In these cases, there was no guarantee that risks would be appropriately identified and assessed, and there was no central point for monitoring outsourcing arrangements.

Fewer than one-third of institutions surveyed had a formal policy on outsourcing. In most cases, banks were able to articulate the types of activities that could be outsourced or the reasons for outsourcing an activity, but this had not been formalised.

Case study 3: Outsourcing unit pricing for managed funds

In 1999, a major Australian institution outsourced its unit pricing and custody arrangements to a custodian which was part of the overall group. The custodian was eventually sold to another party but the outsourcing arrangement remained in place. In January 2004, it was discovered that tax credits had not been claimed for the relevant funds over a number of years and that unit prices had been underestimated as a result. When the problem was discovered, the institution had set to compensate investors, costing approximately AUS$90 million, and the regulators instructed the institution to carry out an overall review of its systems and processes to ensure that the problem does not recur.

Key issues which emerged included:

- There were insufficient controls and checking mechanisms between the third-party provider and the institution.
- The institution was concerned about its ability to easily change processes at the third-party provider as the service level agreements had been negotiated when it was part of the group.
- The organisation was taking a significant reputational risk by outsourcing such an activity to a third-party provider.

Case study 4: OCC action against a bank and service provider

In 2002, the Office of the Comptroller of the Currency (OCC) in the United States took enforcement action against a Californian bank and a third-party service provider to the bank. The service provider originated, serviced and collected certain loans booked by the bank in 18 states and the District of Columbia.

Among other things, the service provider failed to safeguard customer loan files. The files, which represented loans carried on the books of the bank, were discarded in a trash dumpster in 2002.

The OCC alleged that the improper disposal of loan files resulted in violations of laws and regulations.

The OCC also determined that the service provider committed unsafe and unsound practices that included a pattern of following the policies and procedures of the bank and a pattern of mismanagement of the bank's loan files. This case demonstrated the risks national banks expose themselves to when they rent out their charters to third-party vendors and fail to exercise sound oversight.

In the case of the bank, the OCC found that it failed to manage its relationship with the service provider in a safe and sound manner. In addition to violating the Equal Credit Opportunity Act and the Truth in Lending Act, the bank violated safety and soundness standards and also violated the privacy protections of the Gramm-Leach-Bliley Act, which sets standards for safeguarding and maintaining the confidentiality of customer information.

These violations and unsafe and unsound practices led to a cease and desist order against the bank. The order required the bank to pay penalties in civil money and to terminate its relationship with the service provider.

The service provider also paid a sum in penalties and was ordered not to enter into any agreement to provide services to a national bank or its subsidiaries without the approval of the OCC.

To protect the privacy rights of consumers, the order also required the bank to notify all applicants whose loan files were lost. This notification must advise the consumer of any steps they may take to address potential identity theft.

Case study 5: Joint examinations of third-party service providers in the United States

Under the Bank Service Company Act (Act), US Federal Banking Agencies comprising the Federal Regulated Institutions Examination Council (FFIEC)7 have authority to examine banks' third-party service providers. The Act provides that a bank service company (definition includes a Technology Service Provider or TSP) is subject to examination and regulation by the regulator of the bank that is receiving the services. In addition, some FFIEC agencies have taken enforcement actions against TSPs. Following is an example of how the FFIEC agencies have chosen to apply the Act to bank service providers.

A service provider is considered for joint examination if it processes mission-critical applications for a large number of regulated entities that are regulated by more than one agency, thereby posing a high degree of systemic risk; or if the provider processes work from a number of data centres located in different geographic regions. The agencies coordinate on the scope, timing and staffing of these examinations and the resulting examination report is shared with all the member agencies, the examined service provider and its client-regulated entities. The FFIEC agencies use a comprehensive and uniform rating system (referred to as URSIT – Uniform Rating System for Information Technology) to assess and rate IT-related risks of the regulated entities and TSPs. The frequency of IT examinations typically varies between 18 and 36 months based on the risk profile of the TSP. National and regional programmes currently track approximately 160 service providers, and, based upon risk assessments conducted by FFIEC examiners, 130 are examined on a regular basis.

During 2003, the FFIEC member agencies participated jointly in targeted IT examinations of the US regional offices of a global technology service provider. The scope of the risk-focused examinations included activities, transaction processing services, clearing and settlement, information security, business continuity planning and the URSIT components (management, audit, development and acquisition, and support and delivery). In each case, examination findings were published as joint examination reports using the FFIEC's uniform report of examination format for IT examinations at TSPs. The examinations also included limited scope reviews of support activities where the support functions were domiciled outside of the entity's regional primary service centres.

It should be noted that international supervisors have requested access to examination reports on TSPs which provide services to regulated entities in other countries. The issue of sharing reports of examinations resulting from the MDPS programme with international supervisors remains under consideration.

The FFIEC includes the Board of Governors of the Federal Reserve System, the Federal Deposit Insurance Corporation, the National Credit Union Association, the Office of Thrift Supervision and the Office of the Comptroller of the Currency.

Summary

The insource and outsource issues are many and the risks very much depend on the counterparties and even individuals involved in delivering and receiving the services.

Remember that service-level agreements can be both tiresome and costly to monitor and enforce and actually offer little in the way of prevention of operations risk. Compensation may be possible after the event but that does nothing to remove the damage created by loss of reputation for instance.

One thing that is certain about outsourcing is that the risk profile of a firm is altered and becomes much more about another party's abilities in risk management than just the firms. Accountants may make the case financially but in terms of operational risk the advantages of outsourcing are definitely not so clear.

Glossary of risk terminology

Risk	Description	Associated risk type
Accounting Risk	This will occur when a business engages in accounting practices for products or services that are either not suitable, are deliberately misinterpreted or are implemented incorrectly or do not comply with accepted market principles. The risk can also occur if there is doubt about the acceptable accounting standards or where there is conflict between different standards by the setting organisations.	Audit, Regulatory, Reporting
Actioning Risk	The risk of an action being implemented erroneously, accidentally, in unsuitable situations or being authorised or undertaken by unqualified personnel. The risks that arise could create losses (costs, fines, etc.), reputation damage (outcome and impact) and regulatory problems.	Management, Settlement, Payment

Audit Risk	This is the risk that the audit process and people are unable or do not have the ability to, or do not understand sufficiently the processes and procedures being audited.	
Basel II	Inability to demonstrate compliance with the requirement as set out by the Committee of the Bank for International Settlement.	Regulatory
Business Risk	A risk that is derived from the specific services and products and are particular to the industry of the firm concerned. These risks are often subsets of strategic risk and occur or originate from business units.	Operations Risk, Technology Risk, People risk
Business Continuity Risk	The impact of internal or external events that in some way interrupt or curtail the operation of the business for a significant period of time or in some catastrophic financial or logistical way as to make normal or viable operation of business difficult.	Operations Risk Client Risk Counterparty/ Supplier Risk.
Client Risk	The risk of being unable to manage the processes associated with the services provided to clients. Money Laundering Fraud Non-compliance with client regulation (FSA Conduct of Business Rules, etc.) – key areas being suitability (Funds), risk warning distribution, client money/asset segregation	Operations Risk People Risk Regulatory (including fines) Reputation – Loss of clients/ revenue
Competition Risk	A complex risk that can arise in a number of ways and is quite different from business risk, which is about internal decisions and actions.	

	Competition risk could arise from the entrance of a new competitor or product into a market with potential loss of market share and/or increase in investment/costs to compete. This is particularly the case where new competitors cherry-pick profitable market segments, where they have or adapt to new technology and practices quicker, or can respond to changing customer requirements more rapidly. Examples here could be found in e-banking, socially responsible investment products, etc. Competition risk can also apply to prolonged declining market share created by inability to change as well as by poorly managed mergers and takeovers resulting in massive loss of customers that in turn renders the strategic aims unobtainable and is likely to entail severe losses for some period of time	
Compliance Risk	The inability to adequately comply with external regulations or internal rules and controls. This may be caused by lack of knowledge of certain markets, products and regulatory requirements and/or oversight of business units involved	Regulatory Financial
Counterparty Risk	This is the risk associated with dealing with or taking services or products from another party. Includes ingoing support and enhancement of services	Operations Risk
Country Risk	Risk of clearing, settlement and client money regulation not being as strong as in the UK/US Law Infrastructure Information distribution may be less transparent and/or obtainable	Operation Risk Legal Risk

Credit Risk	Risk associated with the default of a counterparty on an obligation	Financial – replacement loss
Creeping Risk	A risk that starts in one part of a business and then moves across and within the business potentially having a greater impact in other areas (similar to a computer virus)	
Custody Risk	The failure to protect assets and any resulting benefits on those assets that are entrusted to the care and safekeeping of the firm	Reputation, Financial, Regulatory
Data Risk	Occurs when data is incorrectly generated, updated, stored or used. Corrupted or incorrect data in critical systems (including risk systems) can have a devastating impact. Unauthorised access, use or publication of confidential client or business data can have such an impact as to put at risk the very existence of the organisation	Technology, Control, Fraud
Demand Risk	A risk where there is uncertainty about future demand for a product caused by uncontrollable or unforeseen changes in the market, for instance regulatory changes. It also manifests itself in situations where there is greater demand than can be satisfied effectively and efficiently, causing delays and penalties to be incurred. Demand risk is relevant in terms of the passing of risk from one business unit to another, that is the aggressive marketing of a product creating risk for the production team (meeting alterations "sold" by the sales team) or client support teams (delays in delivery, quality, etc.).	Strategic, Operational, Operations

Documentation Risk As well as errors within and the ineffectiveness of legal documentation, there is the risk inherent in the publication of documents to clients including correctness of information, suitability of the document (KYC and restricted product docs), confidentiality and frequency requirements (regulatory, agreements, etc.).

Fiduciary Risk Breaching either of the following:

1. A person legally appointed and authorized to hold assets in trust for another person. The fiduciary manages the assets for the benefit of the other person rather than for his or her own profit.
2. A loan made on trust rather than against some security or asset.

Fraud Risk This is the risk that because of weak controls in respect of payments, asset movements, authorisations, access to systems and static data in an organisation, it is vulnerable to an act of fraud by an individual, group of individuals or from external sources

e-banking presents potential for fraud if security over access and data is poor

HR Risk See Personnel Risk

Insource Risk A risk associated with the taking on of additional operational workload with inadequate resource, knowledge and systems

Operations Risk
Financial – compensation for performance
Reputation

Key Performance Indicators (KPI)	Indicators showing a change in performance that may be evidence of increasing or decreasing efficiency and effectiveness of processes and procedures. Often linked into KRIs
Key Risk	Identified as risks that could significantly impact on the achievement of the objectives of a business unit. Likely to be proactively managed by Head of Function/Department on a frequent (i.e. monthly) basis. Typically 15 to 20% of total risks. Firms develop key risk indicators to measure profile changes of the key risks
Key Risk Indicators (KRI)	The identification of risks and their indicators used in the risk management process. It is important that KRIs are monitored for evidence of increasing or decreasing risk levels and also for their continued relevance
Killer Risk	Identified as risks that could significantly impact on the achievement of firm, divisional and/or strategic business unit objectives including a risk whose impact is so severe that it would render the firm incapable of continuing in business or would make the firm so vulnerable that it would be subject to takeover or wipe out by competitors. Typically 2 to 5% of total risks. Managed and tracked through key risk indicators

Know Your Client (KYC)	A risk control measure that demands the organisation has adequate and up-to-date knowledge of the client, its activities, restrictions that apply to the client's actual or potential business and the suitability of products and services marketed and sold to the client.	
Legal Risk	The risk associated with the business of a firm in a jurisdiction. From an operations point of view it would be related to areas such as netting, agreements, claims, etc.	Settlement Risk
Limit Risk	A risk that a control measure is accidentally or deliberately circumvented or is incorrectly set or is not reviewed and amended according to changed circumstances.	
Loss Database	A database that records incidents where a risk event has created a loss at or above a set threshold.	
Management Risk	A risk associated with the failure of management to be structured or operate effectively in relation to the business. Poorly trained, under resourced/overworked or ineffective managers and supervisors are a massive operations risk	Operations Risk Reputation Risk Regulatory Risk
Market Risk	Risk associated with the transactions undertaken by a firm in a market/product. Mainly about price and liquidity but can also be related to other risk like legal and competition	

Money Laundering Risk	A major risk for many organisations that can result in heavy penalties for individuals and loss of authorisation to do business for firms for breaches of the regulations. Any organisation covered by the Regulations must ensure effective controls over possible money laundering including making sure employees are adequately trained	
New Market Risk	This is the risk of operating in a new market environment where knowledge and experience may initially be low. It is also about the risk that procedures and controls are not immediately at the acceptable standard level of existing market usage. Can also apply to activity that is undertaken in emerging markets where the market infrastructure, practices and operation is itself untried and tested	Operations Risk Systems Risk Settlement Risk
New Product Risk	This risk will manifest itself if the launch of or the commencement of trading in a new product or when the launch or use of a new service is undertaken without sufficient infrastructure in place, including controls, systems, knowledge skills, etc.) and prior training of personnel	Operations Risk Systems Risk Settlement Risk
Operational Risk	There are various definitions of operational risk. The Basel Committee defines it as "the risk of loss resulting from inadequate or failed internal processes, people and systems or from external events". Most organizations would add in "loss of reputation".	

Operations Risk	Part of operational risk it applies to the functions that deal with areas like clearing, settlement, payments, delivery of client services, custody, systems, and so on. Operations risk is the failure to provide the required process, procedures and controls for the above.	
Operational Risk Management (ORM)	The process of actively managing operational risks in a structure that adds value as well as reduces potential unnecessary losses. Often run by a Risk Group and usually has one or more operational risk managers in the structure. Likely to include audit and compliance in some capacity	
Operational Risk Officers (OROs)	Name given to a person who is part of the group managing risk and is usually closely related to the business so that they can liaise with both the business and the risk managers on risk issues. Can also be called ORCs – operational risk coordinators	
Outsource Risk	A risk associated with the outsourcing of operational functions and processes. The risk is that you can outsource the function but not the responsibility	Operations Risk Reputation Risk
Payment Risk	A risk associated with the erroneous payment of monies. Often but not always associated with fraud it can be nevertheless a risk that is created by poor training, supervision and procedures for making and/or receiving payments	Fraud Reputation – errors on client accounts

People Risk	This is the risk associated with individuals or teams of people and is often about their potential as a source of risk and also their potential to be a significant contributor to managing some risks like operational risk. One obvious people risk is the level of human error in the processes, the knowledge levels both procedural and business and the ability to work in environments particular to business units, products, services, and so on.	Operations, Financial and Reputation Risk
Personnel Risk	Different from people risk in so much as this may occur because of poor recruitment environments, uncompetitive remuneration, lack of or ineffective training and development, and so on. Loss of key personal is a major personnel risk. Employment Law is also part of this risk and includes areas such as Diversity in the Workplace Directives and training, unfair dismissal, and so on.	Operations, Financial and Reputation Risk
Regulatory Risk	The risk of non-compliance with the regulatory environment where the business is operating, particularly areas such as Authorisation, Marketing and Sales, Conduct of Business, Client relationships, and so on.	
Risk Event	The occurrence of a possible risk situation becoming an actual risk situation with resultant actual impact.	

Standard Risk A risk that is identified and managed as part of the day-to-day business process by the boys and girls doing their jobs effectively and efficiently.

Controls devised and implemented by managers and supervisors in the business.

Monitored by risk managers from management information provided by the business but essentially not what the risk managers or OROs should be focussing on

Strategic Risk A risk that is associated with decisions and leadership, that is the adoption of a working practice that is old, untried or ill thought out that results in unnecessary pressure, workloads, costs and falling performance of people, systems and the business

Technology Risk The risk associated with the use of technology in a firm

Most obvious risks are:

1. lack of knowledge of systems
2. inability to manage projects
3. lack of support for systems
4. lack of awareness of systems capability and scope
5. inappropriate systems for the business
6. old and outdated technology
7. access – hackers and viruses, malicious attack.

Value At Risk (VAR) A technique used to estimate the probability of portfolio losses based on the statistical analysis of historical price trends and volatilities.

Workflow Risk Risk associated with workflow and processes covering:

1. variable flow
2. under-resourcing
3. pressure points
4. disruption
5. lack of knowledge
6. unnecessary complex procedures
7. poor technology
8. lack of STP
9. cross-border processes
10. data sources.

This glossary of terms is compiled from various sources and is believed to be correct although no responsibility can be taken for any errors or omissions. We would recommend the following publications and websites for further information concerning risk sources, definitions, controls and risk management.

Publications

Measuring and Managing Operational Risks in Financial Institutions
Christopher Marshall published by Wiley

*Controls, Procedures and Risk
David Loader published by Butterworth Heinemann

*Advanced Operations Management
David Loader published by Wiley/The Securities Institute

*Regulation and Compliance in Operations
David Loader published by Butterworth Heinemann

*Glossary of Financial Market Terms
Published by the dsc.portfolio

Against The Gods –The Remarkable Story of Risk
Peter L Bernstein published by Wiley

Useful websites

www.issanet.org	(International Securities Services Association)
www.fsa.gov.uk	(Financial Services Authority)
www.sii.org.uk	(The Securities and Investment Institute)
www.isma.co.uk	(International Securities Markets Association)
www.bis.org	(Bank for International Settlement)
www.cls-group.com	(CLS Bank)
www.isda.org	(International Swaps and Derivatives Association)
www.isla.co.uk	(International Securities Lending Association)
www.bba.org.uk	(British Bankers Association)
www.foa.org.uk	(Futures and Options Association)

Appendix 1: Consolidated KYC risk management

Basel Commitee
on Banking Supervision

Consultative Document

Consolidated KYC
Risk Management

Issued for comment by
30 October 2003

August 2003

BANK FOR INTERNATIONAL SETTLEMENTS

Table of Contents

Introduction

1. The adoption of effective know-your-customer (KYC) standards is an essential part of banks' risk management practices. As discussed in the *Customer due diligence for banks*[1] (CDD) paper, banks with inadequate KYC standards may be subject to significant risks, especially legal and reputational risk. Sound KYC policies and procedures not only contribute to a bank's overall safety and soundness, they also protect the integrity of the banking system by reducing the likelihood of banks becoming vehicles for money laundering, terrorist financing and other unlawful activities.
2. The CDD paper outlines four essential elements necessary for a sound KYC programme. These elements are: (i) customer acceptance policy; (ii) customer identification; (iii) on-going monitoring of higher risk accounts; and (iv) risk management. To be truly effective, these elements should be adopted on a consolidated basis, encompassing the parent bank or head office[2] and all foreign branches and subsidiaries.
3. Jurisdictions should facilitate consolidated KYC risk management by providing an appropriate legal framework which allows the cross-border sharing of information. Legal restrictions that impede effective consolidated KYC risk management processes should be removed.
4. A global risk management programme for KYC should incorporate consistent identification and monitoring of customer accounts globally across business lines and geographical locations, as well as oversight at the parent level, in order to capture instances and

[1] Basel Committee on Banking Supervision, October 2001.
[2] The term "head office" is used subsequently in this document to refer also to the parent bank.

patterns of unusual[3] transactions that might otherwise go undetected. Such comprehensive treatment of customer information can significantly contribute to a bank's overall reputational, concentration, operational and legal risk management through the detection of potentially harmful activities.

5. This paper describes the critical elements for effective consolidated KYC risk management.

Global process for managing KYC risks

6. The four essential elements of a sound KYC programme should be fully incorporated into a bank's risk management and control procedures to ensure that all aspects of KYC risk are identified and can be appropriately mitigated. Hence, a bank should aim to apply its customer acceptance policy, procedures for customer identification, process for monitoring higher risk accounts and risk management framework on a global basis to all of its branches and subsidiaries around the world. The bank should clearly communicate those policies and procedures and ensure that they are fully adhered to. Where the minimum KYC standards of the home and host countries differ, offices in host jurisdictions should apply the higher standard of the two (CDD paragraph 66).

Customer acceptance policy

7. Banks should develop clear customer acceptance policies and procedures that include guidance on the types of customers that are likely to pose a higher than average risk to the bank (CDD paragraph 20), including managerial review of such prospective customers where appropriate. These policies and procedures for customer acceptance should be implemented consistently throughout the organisation.

Customer identification

8. A bank should establish a systematic procedure for identifying new customers (CDD paragraph 22). It should develop standards on what records are to be obtained and retained for customer identification on a global basis, including enhanced due diligence requirements for higher risk customers.

[3] The term "unusual" is used in this paper to refer also to "suspicious".

9. A bank should obtain appropriate identification information and maintain such information in a readily retrievable format so as to adequately identify its customers[4], as well as fulfil any local reporting requirements. Relevant information should be accessible for purposes of information sharing among the banking group's head office, branches and subsidiaries.
10. Each office of the banking group should be in a position to comply with minimum identification and accessibility standards applied by the head office. However, some differences in information collection and retention may be necessary across jurisdictions to conform to local requirements or relative risk factors.

Monitoring of accounts and transactions

11. An essential element for addressing higher risks is the monitoring of customer account activity on a worldwide basis, regardless of whether the accounts are held on- or off-balance sheet, as assets under management, or on a fiduciary basis (CDD paragraph 16). Two of the approaches by which such monitoring may be accomplished are (1) the use of a centralised database; and (2) decentralised databases with robust information sharing between the head office and its branches and subsidiaries.
12. Under the first approach, accounts are monitored through the use of centralised databases of account balances, account activity and payments. This approach offers the advantage of permitting local and centralised monitoring across accounts in each office of the bank and facilitates monitoring of inter-office activity of customers with accounts in more than one office. However, because many foreign jurisdictions do not permit the routine transmission of customer data outside of their jurisdiction this approach may have limited applicability. An example of this practice can be seen in banks' monitoring of global payment activity, which has been facilitated by the establishment of centralised processing sites, i.e. payment "hubs".
13. Under the second approach, each office maintains and monitors information on its accounts and transactions. In this decentralised approach, local monitoring should be complemented by a robust process of information sharing between the head office and its branches and subsidiaries regarding accounts and activity

[4] See customer identification requirements in *Guidance to Account Opening and Customer Identification*, an attachment to the Basel Committee's *Customer due diligence for banks* (October 2001) paper.

that may represent heightened risk. Information should flow both ways. Whilst the head office should inform the foreign branch or subsidiary of higher risk customers, the foreign branch or subsidiary should likewise be able to inform proactively the head office of higher risk relationships and other events that are relevant to the global management of reputational, legal, concentration and operational risk.

14. Regardless of the approach taken, banks should have policies and procedures for monitoring account activity for unusual transactions that are applied on a global basis. The procedures should be risk-based and emphasise the need to monitor both intra- and inter-country account activities.

Consolidated risk management and information sharing

15. KYC risk management programmes should include proper management oversight, systems and controls, segregation of duties, training and other related policies (CDD paragraph 55). The risk management programme should be implemented on a global basis. Explicit responsibility should be allocated within the bank for ensuring that the bank's policies and procedures for the risk management programme are managed effectively and are, at a minimum, in accordance with the bank's global standards for customer identification, ongoing monitoring of accounts and transactions and the sharing of information.
16. Banks should ensure that their subsidiary and branch networks proactively provide information concerning higher risk customers and activities relevant to the global management of reputational, legal, concentration and operational risks, and respond to head office requests for account information in a timely manner. The bank's policies and procedures should describe the process to be followed for investigating and reporting unusual activity.
17. For information that is reported to the head office by a branch or subsidiary, head office should assess its world-wide exposure to the customer, and should have policies and procedures for ascertaining whether other branches or subsidiaries hold accounts for the same party and assessing the group-wide reputational, legal, concentration and operational risks. The bank should also have procedures governing global account relationships that are deemed unusual, detailing escalation procedures and guidance on restricting activities, including the closing of accounts as appropriate.

18. In addition to the proactive consolidated risk management processes, banks and their local offices should be responsive to requests from their respective law enforcement authorities for information about account holders that is needed in the authorities' effort to combat money laundering and the financing of terrorism. Head office should be able to require all offices to search their files against a list of individuals or organisations suspected of aiding and abetting terrorist financing or money laundering, and report matches.
19. Banks' compliance and internal audit staffs, or external auditors, should evaluate adherence to all aspects of the global standards for KYC, including the requirements for sharing information with head office and responding to queries from head office related to higher risk and unusual account activities. The banking group's internal audit and compliance functions are the principal mechanism for monitoring the application of the bank's global KYC policies and procedures, including the effectiveness of the procedures for sharing information within the group
20. Where overseas offices are faced with host country laws that prevent compliance with the KYC standards of the home country, those offices should ensure that the head office and its home country supervisor are fully informed of the nature of the difference. Regarding such jurisdictions, banks should be aware of the higher reputational risk of conducting business in them, and should have a procedure for reviewing the vulnerability of the individual operating units, and implement additional safeguards where appropriate, including the possibility of closing down the operation (CDD paragraph 69).

Mixed financial groups

21. Many banking groups now engage in securities and insurance businesses. Customer due diligence by mixed financial groups poses issues that may not be present for a pure banking group. Mixed groups should have systems and processes in place to monitor and share information on the identity of customers and account activity of the entire group, and to be alert to customers that use their services in different sectors. A customer relationship issue that arises in one part of a group would affect the reputation risk of the whole group.
22. While variations in the nature of activities, and patterns of relationships between institutions and customers in each sector

justify variations in the KYC requirements imposed on each sector, the group should be alert when cross-selling products and services to customers from different business arms that the KYC requirements of the relevant sectors should be applied.

The role of the supervisor

23. Supervisors should verify that appropriate internal controls for KYC are in place and that banks are in compliance with supervisory and regulatory guidance. The supervisory process should include not only a review of policies and procedures but also a review of customer files and the sampling of some accounts (CDD paragraph 61).
24. In a cross-border context, home country supervisors or auditors should face no impediments in verifying the unit's compliance with KYC policies and procedures during onsite inspections. This will require a review of customer files and some random sampling of accounts. Home country supervisors should have access to information on sampled individual customer accounts to the extent necessary to enable a proper evaluation of the application of KYC standards and an assessment of risk management practices, and should not be impeded by local bank secrecy laws. In the case of branches or subsidiaries of international banking groups, while the home country supervisor is responsible for consolidated supervision of compliance with global KYC policies and procedures, the host country supervisor retains responsibility for the supervision of compliance with local KYC regulations.
25. The role of internal audit is particularly important in the evaluation of adherence to KYC standards on a consolidated basis and home country supervisors should ensure that they have effective access to any relevant reports carried out by internal audit.
26. Safeguards are needed to ensure that information regarding individual accounts is used exclusively for lawful supervisory purposes, and can be protected by the recipient in a satisfactory manner. A statement of mutual cooperation to facilitate information sharing between the two supervisors would be helpful in this regard (CDD paragraph 68).

Appendix 2: A collection of excerpts and published operational risk guidelines and recommendations

Derivatives

The following is an extract from the Futures and Options Association publication.

Managing Derivatives Risk – Guidelines for End Users of Derivatives

Principle 5: Operational Risk

Senior management should ensure that procedures and controls for derivatives are in place to identify, measure, manage, monitor, report on and, where practical, mitigate operational risk, including technological risk.

5.1 Operational Risk is defined as the risk of direct or indirect loss resulting from inadequate or failed internal processes, people and systems or from external events (The New Basel Capital Accord, 2001).

5.2 Senior management should have oversight responsibility to identify and analyse all types of existing and potential operational risks faced by the organisation, which may arise from, for example:

(a) the introduction and development of new products;
(b) changes in management and/or the organization's operations;
(c) the management of third parties, particularly in the context of the outsourcing and procurement of IT services;
(d) the development, introduction, security and use (and failure) of automated systems, particularly in relation to key business processes;
(e) human resource failures, particularly as regards people-related processes such as recruitment and training of staff;
(f) any loss in business continuity due to events such as natural disasters, terrorist acts;
(g) changes in regulatory and/or legal environment. (See further Principle 6 "Managing Legal and Documentation Risk".)

5.3 Having identified and analysed areas of potential operational risks, senior management should ensure that appropriate internal controls and procedures are established to measure, manage, monitor, mitigate and report on such risks on a continuing basis, including:

(a) setting risk indicators and limits for operational areas (e.g. to ensure senior managers are advised of any escalation in risk);
(b) carrying out independent internal audits to assure management of the adequacy and effectiveness of the organisation's controls and procedures;
(c) ensuring segregation of duties, confirmations and reconciliations, reporting and monitoring. For example, individuals responsible for entering into derivatives transactions should be segregated from those responsible for transaction processing, calculating profit and loss, monitoring risk, performing reconciliations and transactional reporting;
(d) timely reporting covering:
  (i) details of authorised and unauthorised changes in and/or access to IT systems;
  (ii) information on staff issues, e.g. turnover rates, disciplinary events and changes in individual responsibilities;
  (iii) trading activities (see paras 3.9 to 3.11).

IT Systems Management

5.4 Computer systems used for the initial recording, processing, valuing and risk modelling of derivatives transactions should be subject to the same procedures and controls as other systems used by the organisation. In particular, there should be a systems outline that sets out how the systems used for any process within the life cycle of a derivatives trade are controlled. Any such outline should include:

(a) systems and data architecture, setting out the interfaces between the various systems;

(b) clear levels of responsibility have been assigned, particularly over systems development, system operation, technical support and security administration;

(c) logical access to system programs and data is limited to authorised individuals (including the use of firewalls and encryption technology where the organisation is connected to the external environment); and access violation attempts are monitored and reported;

(d) physical access to computer equipment, storage media and programme documentation is limited to authorised individuals through the use of appropriate security devices;

(e) estimations are made (and periodically reviewed) of current and future systems capacity, based on current utilisation levels and anticipated growth rates, to ensure that adequate processing and capacity continues to be available at each processing location;

(f) systems processing is scheduled appropriately and deviations are identified and resolved in a timely manner;

(g) systems disaster recovery plans are developed, updated and tested regularly to enable the organisation to recover systems and data in a timely manner, and aligned to the organisation's business continuity plans;

(h) clear change control procedures are in place and adhered to when system developments, modifications and testing are being made.

In cases where spreadsheets and/or manual workarounds are used for reports (for example, for position keeping or valuation), procedures should be developed to ensure that access is carefully controlled and the spreadsheets are used only for their intended purpose. In addition, independent validation of the models underlying the spreadsheets and/or manual workarounds should be carried out to ensure that these models are tested, reliable and consistent with the standards of external models.

5.5 An organisation should ensure that its business strategy is translated into specific system requirements so that systems needs can be analysed and specified and appropriate systems selected. Once specified, design and development activity should ensure that systems are developed to a consistent standard and that systems documentation provides for long-term support and maintenance. Successful implementation of systems requires adequate testing, quality assurance, change controls and project management to ensure that systems meet business requirements on time and within budget. In addition, the development, planning and testing of contingency and disaster recovery strategies are crucial to ensure the timely recovery of key business processes and supporting systems.

Use of Electronic Order Routing Systems

5.6 Derivatives transactions are increasingly being conducted electronically and more and more business operations are able to process transactions from start to finish with minimal manual intervention. Direct connectivity with third parties (such as brokers) through the use of electronic order routing systems (EORS) is now commonplace. Although use of these systems can deliver many advantages to the end-user (e.g. more cost efficient and rapid transaction processing), dealing activities must be monitored closely to ensure that transactions are processed completely, accurately, on time and without duplication. It is also vital that controls are built into the systems covering, for example, trade input, verification and release to minimise errors and unauthorised trading. Management should also be able to access real time information about the precise status of each transaction and monitoring systems should be capable of providing early warning of potential difficulties in processing.

Given the extent of and the degree of reliance based upon automation, all electronic systems should be subject to thorough testing prior to implementation. Examples of the kind of vital checks that should be made before and while using such systems are included in the suggested action points at the end of this Chapter.

5.7 When using EORS, due attention should be given to the following:

(a) Lack of compatibility – the organisation must ensure that it meets the IT hardware specifications and network configuration recommended by the EORS provider, as this can directly affect the EORS's performance;

(b) Adequate training – the organisation should ensure that all EORS users are aware that efficient performance can be inhibited by their own activities e.g. running additional software applications on dedicated EORS hardware. As a result, reference to best practice user guides issued by the EORS provider is essential. The effective communication of these best practice criteria to EORS users through training will help maximise EORS's performance;

(c) Security risk – the EORS provider will accept no liability for a systems failure that results from the introduction of viruses or similar items by an employee of the organisation (and may hold the organisation liable and seek appropriate damages). The organisation must ensure therefore that it has adequate procedures in place to raise awareness of the dangers of viruses and to minimise the risks of their introduction into the system. Security features should be in place to restrict trading access to authorised personnel only (e.g. through the use of user names and passwords) and there should be procedures for managing access to and invalidating codes when authorised personnel leave the organisation;

(d) Systems failure and contingency arrangements – in the event of a systems failure, the organisation must ensure that it can swiftly access alternative mechanisms to support its trading activities. Particular care should be taken to check whether individual orders were executed prior to the systems failure before re-entering them via the back-up system;

(e) Incorrect or erroneous orders – directly inputting orders via an EORS exposes the organisation to potential losses where orders are incorrectly submitted to the exchange's central order book. To minimise these risks, it is vital that authorised personnel are properly trained in the use of the EORS and are aware of the procedure for correcting/amending incorrectly or erroneously entered orders.

5.8 When accessing a derivatives exchange electronically, an organisation must ensure that it is able to comply with both the letter and the spirit of that exchange's rules and regulations. The organisation must therefore have procedures in place whereby all employees authorised to use an EORS become familiar with and are able to access directly all applicable rules and regulations and any changes that may be introduced to those rules and regulations.

Third Party Dependencies[5]

5.9 An organisation may choose to outsource part of its support activities with a view to focusing on its core business activities, realising cost benefits, transferring risks and streamlining operations. Where the organisation carries out similar operational activities in a number of locations, it may also be beneficial to establish a central shared service to achieve economies of scale and the resulting cost efficiencies. The operational risks associated with outsourcing and shared services, however, need to be carefully managed by clearly defining measurable services, allocating responsibilities and accountabilities, and establishing contracts and service levels.

Professional Expertise and Human Resources

5.10 The level of expertise of managers and supervisors should be reviewed regularly by senior management or by the board of directors (or a sub-committee) to satisfy themselves that undue reliance is not being placed on a few specialists, or even a sole specialist. Staff changes and turnover can place an organisation at risk, so contingency plans should be made for such circumstances. This may include the periodic rotation of staff who undertake key functions, management succession, planning for key members of management and appropriate measures to mitigate the risk of loss of these personnel.

5.11 All personnel should fully understand their responsibilities, their reporting lines and the processes and procedures to which they are subject. This can be achieved by defining the scope of their responsibilities within documented job descriptions and procedures, and linking these to the performance appraisal process. These documents should be reviewed and updated on a timely basis.

5.12 An organisation's human resources department should work closely with all areas of the business to ensure that only suitable individuals are employed. Individuals involved in transactions (including those who manage risk, as well as their supervisors,

[5] The FOA has produced separate Guidelines for the Procurement and Outsourcing of IT Services, which are available from the FOA (full details are given on the website, www.foa.co.uk).

and those responsible for assessing, reporting, controlling and providing required IT and auditing those activities) should be appropriately trained and have adequate knowledge and experience.

Managers should understand not only the nature of the instruments but the broader business context in which they are used.

To ensure that individuals are properly informed and the organisation's risk management objectives are continually and appropriately aligned with individual objectives, individual training needs should be identified and met on a regular basis. Manager and staff training in technical and quantitative risk management skills should be complemented by training in other skills, such as project and people management, in order to build effective teams. This could include attendance at external courses, in-house training sessions and reading reference books.

5.13 Incentives should be developed to encourage voluntary disclosure of transactions which breach limits or pre-authorisation requirements and there should be an appropriate disciplinary framework for dealing with deliberate or consistent breaches.

Business Continuity Planning

5.14 Organisations should develop, test and keep under regular review contingency plans so that they can continue their activities (e.g. bearing in mind the speed with which prices can move, the ability to close out positions quickly) in the event of an operational failure on the part of the organisation itself (e.g. a failure of computer system) or resulting from an external problem (e.g. a systems breakdown, loss of key personnel, a failure of a third party (including brokers)) and, as necessary, move to alternative premises. For example, an organisation should ensure that its brokers are operational, that temporary offices have been identified, and all relevant IT and support functions are in working order. The organisation may wish to ensure also that its brokers have suitable and sufficient emergency switching facilities with appropriate brokers.

Reputational Risk

5.15 While reputational risk is often excluded from the definition of operational risk (for example, the New Basle Capital Accord excludes reputational risk for the purpose of calculating capital requirements), recent headline cases such as those involving lack of accounting transparency shows that any form of adverse publicity or perception about the organisation (whether justified or not) which damages its reputation can increase significantly its risk and/or its cost base in some of its key activities resulting in, for example, the withdrawal of credit lines, loss of customers, loss of key staff, the impact of tighter regulatory controls, loss of investment confidence and withdrawal of third party suppliers.

5.16 In such circumstances, there has to be careful management of any contact with press, the development of an informed working relationship with any relevant regulatory authority and a very close focus on retaining the goodwill and support of customers and suppliers. Aside from general matters of administration and normal communications, contact should be restricted to or managed centrally by senior managers during the time of crisis.

Suggested Action Points

- *Management reports should be distributed to the appropriate senior managers/directors on a timely basis and contain relevant, reliable and comprehensible information;*
- *Computer systems should be examined to ensure that they are adequate and robust, independently reviewed and subject to controls to ensure amendments to programmes are adequate;*
- *The level of expertise in the organisation should be reviewed to ensure that there is no undue reliance on too few specialists;*
- *When using an EORS, an organisation should:*
  - *ensure that the PC hardware specification meets the provider's requirements;*
  - *ensure that any supporting hardware provided by the EORS provider is maintained in accordance with the provider's specifications;*
  - *ensure that the internal network configuration meets the provider's requirements;*
  - *where necessary, impose restrictions on running additional applications on dedicated EORS hardware;*
  - *impose appropriate security safeguards to prevent the introduction of viruses;*

- *ensure that, in the event of failure of the EORS, appropriate back-up arrangements are available and accessible within a short time-frame;*
- *if the EORS provider does not provide a help desk service, ensure that a similar support function is available to deal with internal enquiries.*

- *Contingency plans should be formulated and documented to ensure the continuance of trading activities in emergency situations and reviewed regularly to make sure they are capable of implementation. They should be monitored to ensure that they continue to reflect current activity, tested to confirm their effectiveness and are properly understood by key personnel.*

About the FOA

The Futures and Options Association (www.foa.co.uk)

The FOA is an industry trade association for firms and institutions carrying on business in futures, options and other derivatives or which use such products in their business. It covers the whole spectrum of financial, metal, "soft" commodity and energy products. Its principal role is:

"To represent the interests of its members in the public and regulatory domain and deliver a wide range of support services to the membership."

The FOA fulfils this role by:

- constructive liaison with regulators, government and other political and trade bodies at national, European and international levels;
- raising public awareness and understanding of the derivatives industry;
- producing standardised industry documentation, publications and guidelines;
- delivering training courses and workshops.

Further information on the FOA can be obtained from its website (www.foa.co.uk).

Appendix 3: Global clearing and settlement – The G30 twenty recommendations

CREATING A STRENGTHNED INTEROPERABLE GLOBAL NETWORK

1. Eliminate paper and automate communication, data capture and enrichment
2. Harmonise messaging standards and communication protocols
3. Develop and implement reference data standards
4. Synchronize timing between different clearing and settlement systems and associated payment and foreign-exchange systems
5. Automate and standardise institutional trade matching
6. Expand the use of central counterparties
7. Permit securities lending and borrowing to expedite settlement
8. Automate and standardise asset servicing processes, including corporate actions, tax relief arrangements and restrictions on foreign ownerships

MITIGATING RISK

9. Ensure the financial integrity of providers of clearing and settlement services
10. Reinforce the risk management practices of users of clearing and settlement service providers

11. Ensure final, simultaneous transfer and availability of assets
12. Ensure effective business continuity and disaster recovery planning
13. Address the possibility of failure of a systemically important institution
14. Strengthen assessment of enforceability of contracts
15. Advance legal certainty over rights to securities, cash or collateral
16. Recognise and support improved valuation and closeout netting arrangements

IMPROVING GOVERNANCE

17. Ensure appointment of appropriately experienced and senior board members
18. Promote fair access to securities clearing and settlement networks
19. Ensure equitable and effective attention to stakeholders interests
20. Encourage consistent regulation and oversight of securities clearing and settlement service providers

Published 2003, the full document can be obtained from www.group30.org

Managing Operational Risk

Outsourcing in Financial Services

Executive Summary

Financial services businesses throughout the world are increasingly using third parties to carry out activities that the businesses themselves would normally have undertaken. Industry research and surveys by regulators show financial firms outsourcing significant parts of their regulated and unregulated activities. These outsourcing arrangements are also becoming increasingly complex.

Outsourcing has the potential to transfer risk, management and compliance to third parties who may not be regulated, and who may operate offshore. In these situations, how can financial service businesses remain confident that they remain in charge of their own business and in control of their business risks? How do they know they are complying with their regulatory responsibilities? How can these businesses demonstrate that they are doing so when regulators ask?

To help answer these questions and to guide regulated businesses, the Joint Forum established a working group to develop high-level principles about outsourcing. In this paper, the key issues and risks are spelt out in more detail and principles are put forward that can serve as benchmarks. The principles apply across the banking, insurance and securities sectors, and the international committees involved in each sector may build on these principles to offer more specific and focused guidance. Selected international case studies (see Annex A) show why these questions matter.

Today outsourcing is increasingly used as a means of both reducing costs and achieving strategic aims. Its potential impact can be seen across many business activities, including information technology (e.g., applications development, programming, and coding), specific operations (e.g., some aspects of finance and accounting, back-office activities and processing, and administration), and contract functions (e.g., call centres). Industry reports and regulatory surveys of industry practice indicate that financial firms are entering into arrangements in which other firms – related firms within a corporate group and third-party service providers – conduct significant parts of the enterprise's regulated and unregulated activities.

Activities and functions within an organisation are performed and delivered in diverse ways. An institution might split such functions as product manufacturing, marketing, back-office and distribution within the regulated entity. Where a regulated entity keeps such arrangements inhouse, but operates some activities from various locations, this would not be classified as outsourcing. The entity would therefore be expected to provide for any risks posed by this in its regular risk management framework.

Increasingly more complex arrangements are developing whereby related entities perform some activities, while unrelated service providers perform others. In each case the service provider may or may not be a regulated entity. The Joint Forum principles are designed to apply whether or not the service provider is a regulated entity.

Outsourcing has been identified in various industry and regulatory reports as raising issues related to risk transfer and management, frequently on a cross-border basis, and industry and regulators acknowledge that this increased reliance on the outsourcing of activities may impact on the ability of regulated entities to manage their risks and monitor their compliance with regulatory requirements. Additionally, there is concern among regulators as to how outsourcing potentially could impede the ability of regulated entities to demonstrate to regulators (e.g., through examinations) that they are taking appropriate steps to manage their risks and comply with applicable regulations.

Among the specific concerns raised by outsourcing activities is the potential for over-reliance on outsourced activities that are critical to the ongoing viability of a regulated entity as well as its obligations to customers.

Regulated entities can mitigate these risks by taking steps (as discussed in the principles) to: draw up comprehensive and clear outsourcing policies, establish effective risk management programmes, require contingency planning by the outsourcing firm, negotiate appropriate outsourcing contracts, and analyse the financial and infrastructure resources of the service provider.

Regulators can also mitigate concerns by ensuring that outsourcing is adequately considered in their assessments of individual firms whilst taking account of concentration risks in thirdparty providers when considering systemic risk issues.

Of particular interest to regulators is the preservation at the regulated entity of strong corporate governance. In this regard outsourcing activities that may impede an outsourcing firm's management from fulfilling its regulatory responsibilities are of concern to regulators. The rapid rate of IT innovation, along with an increasing reliance on external service providers have the potential of leading to systemic problems unless appropriately constrained by a combination of market and regulatory influences.

This paper attempts to spell out these concerns in more detail and develop a set of principles that gives guidance to firms, and to regulators, to help them better mitigate these concerns without hindering the efficiency and effectiveness of firms.

The full document is to be found at the BIS website – www.bis.org

FX Settlement Risk

CLS Bank

With the average daily turnover in global FX transactions at over US$2 trillion, the FX market has long needed an effective cross-currency settlement process. And while transaction volumes have increased, the way in which they're settled has stayed virtually the same for 300 years.

Before CLS, each side of a trade was paid separately. Taking time-zone differences into account, this heightened the risk of one party defaulting.

CLS is a response to regulatory concern about systematic risk. It eliminates that 'temporal' settlement risk, making same-day settlement both possible *and final.*

CLS provides and is developing multiple commercial benefits. These include opportunities to deal with trading counter-parties, reduce costly reconciliation, and exploit the real-time information on currency cycling and settlement that CLS can provide.

Why CLS?

With the average daily turnover in global FX transactions at almost US$2 trillion, the FX market has long needed an effective cross-currency settlement process.

And while transaction volumes have increased, the way in which they're settled has stayed virtually the same for 300 years.

Before CLS, each side of a trade was paid separately. Taking time-zone differences into account, this heightened the risk of one party defaulting.

CLS is a response to regulatory concern about systematic risk. It eliminates that 'temporal' settlement risk, making same-day settlement both possible *and final.*

And as CLS evolves, our customers are developing multiple commercial benefits. These include opportunities to deal with trading counter-parties, reduce costly reconciliation, and exploit the real-time information on currency cycling and settlement that only CLS can provide.

How CLS works

The CLS settlement process

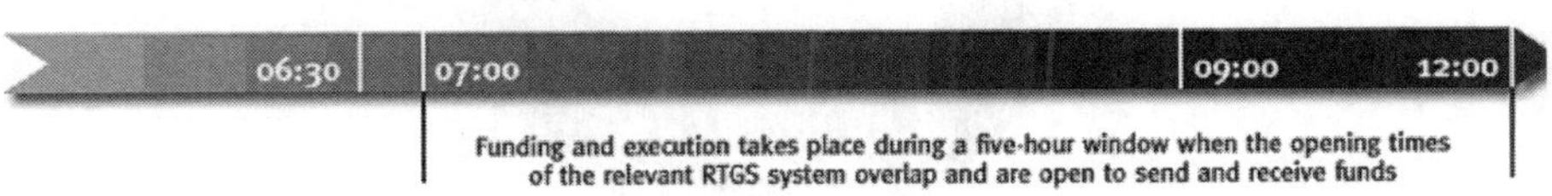

Submitting instructions

» Up until 06:30 CET, Settlement Members can submit settlement instructions directly to CLS Bank for processing.

» At 06:30 each Settlement Member receives its final pay-in schedule for the day.

Banks can review net pay-in totals at any time before the settlement day, so they have a window on the day's transactions.

Because payments are made on the net position for each currency (rather than on a gross transaction-by-transaction basis), CLS reduces the funding necessary for the gross total individual instructions by up to 90%.

Settlement and funding

» Settlement Members pay in the net funds at the relevant central banks.

» Once the first funding is paid in, the settlement execution cycle starts at 07:00 CET.

Banks receive real-time information and manage their own data. Tracking operational errors reduces costly reconciliation delays.

Banks can leverage values in any currency to settle other currencies, as long as they maintain an overall positive account balance.

Execution

» Between 07:00 and 09:00 CET, CLS Bank continuously receives funds from Settlement Members, settles instructions across its books, and pays out funds to Settlement Members – until all instructions are settled.

» Trades that can't immediately settle are put back in the queue and continually revisited until they settle.

CLS checks that each Settlement Member has a net positive balance across all currencies (after market volatility haircuts), ensuring that CLS Bank and its Settlement Members are protected.

» Between 09:00 and 12.00 CET, the pay-ins and pay-outs are finalised.

» If there are no problems by 12:00 CET, all funds will have been disbursed back to Settlement Members.

If the strict settlement criteria aren't met for each side of a trade, the instructions to CLS Bank don't settle and no funds are exchanged.

CLS is a real-time system that enables simultaneous settlement globally, irrespective of time zones.

CLS is an ongoing process of:

- submitting instructions – receiving payments of specified currencies from customers
- funding – settling pairs of instructions that satisfy all criteria
- execution – making pay-outs in specified currencies.

Settlement is final and irrevocable or funds are returned same day.

Participating banks get real-time settlement information that helps them to manage liquidity more efficiently, reduce credit risks and introduce operational efficiencies.

This is all done within a *five-hour window, which represents the overlapping business hours of the participating settlement systems.

CLS in business

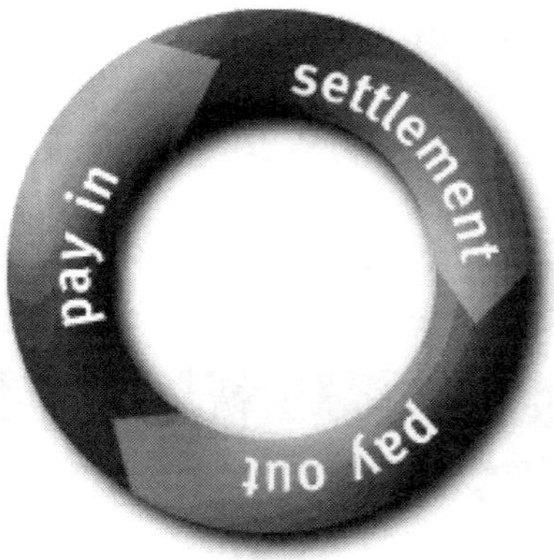

For the trading desk

- Traders can expand their FX business with counterparty banks without increasing limits.
- Institutions have fewer reservations about transacting in CLS currencies.

For treasury and cash managers

- Managers have more certainty about intraday and end-of-day cash positions.
- Global settlement can rationalise nostro accounts and leverage multi-currency accounts.

*three hours in Asia Pacific

For risk managers

- Risk managers keep control of funds for longer.
- The volume and overall value of payments is reduced, as are cash-clearing costs.
- Costly errors are minimised and any problems can be resolved fast.

Who is involved

CLS is only available through the unique and regulated relationship between CLS Bank, the central banks in whose currencies CLS settles, and members of CLS Bank.

The CLS process involves a number of different parties:

- shareholders
- Members – either Settlement Members or User Members
- third parties.

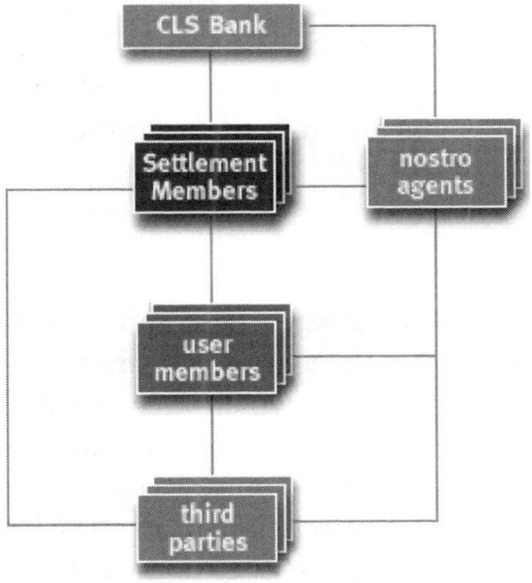

Shareholders

CLS Bank is owned by nearly 70 of the world's largest financial groups throughout the US, Europe and Asia Pacific. Between them, our shareholders are responsible for more than half the value transferred in the world's FX market. Five CLS shareholders alone represent over 44% of this market. Our shareholders have invested in CLS to develop CLS settlement. Each has purchased an equal shareholding in the CLS Group of companies. Each shareholder has the exclusive right to become a CLS Bank Settlement Member with direct access to the CLS system.

Settlement Members

A Settlement Member must be a shareholder of CLS Group and must show that they have the financial and operational capability and sufficient liquidity to support their financial commitments to CLS. They can each submit settlement instructions directly to CLS Bank and receive information on the status of their instructions. Each Settlement Member has a multi-currency account with CLS Bank, with the ability to move funds. Settlement Members have direct access and input deals on their own behalf and on behalf of their customers. They can provide a branded CLS service to their third-party customers as part of their agreement with CLS Bank.

User Members

User Members can submit settlement instructions for themselves and their customers. However, User Members do not have an account with CLS Bank. Instead they are sponsored by a Settlement Member who acts on their behalf. Each instruction submitted by a user member must be authorised by a designated Settlement Member. The instruction is then eligible for settlement through the account Settlement Member's account.

Third parties

Third parties are customers of settlement and user members and have no direct access to CLS. Settlement or user members must handle all instructions and financial flows, which are consolidated in CLS. The terms on which members can act on behalf of third parties are governed by private arrangement. These do not directly involve CLS Bank and third parties do not have any relationship with CLS Bank. Members may provide a trademarked CLS service to their third-party customers. You can find out more about Settlement Members' customers here.

Nostro agents

Nostro agents:

- receive payment instructions from Settlement Members
- may have multiple relationships with Settlement Members
- must provide time-sensitive fund transfers to Settlement Members' accounts at CLS Bank
- receive funds from CLS Bank, User Members, third parties and others for credit to the Settlement Member account.

Settlement Members' customers

Most of the beneficiaries of CLS are third parties who participate indirectly as customers of Settlement Members. In turn, some third parties are offering CLS services to their customers.

There are three types of CLS third party:

- third-party banks
- fund managers
- non-bank financial institutions and corporates.

Third-party banks

Many medium-sized and large banks, including some high-volume trading organisations, have announced that they're becoming third-party users of CLS. Others in the developing markets have recognised the benefits of a common settlement system.

Fund managers

CLS can settle FX trades for both treasury and securities clearing and the next wave of CLS participants will be fund managers including pension funds and asset management divisions of banks and insurance companies, as well as investment managers. Fund managers will benefit significantly from CLS following the introduction of a unique solution – *Enhanced Fund FX* – that enables fund managers to eliminate FX settlement risk associated with FX deals for cross-border investment or hedging.

Non-bank financial institutions and corporates

Non-banking and corporate organisations have tended to trade with one or a very limited number of dealer banks that net settlement obligations through a concentration account. When they use CLS, these organisations get the opportunity to rationalise their back-office process, optimise their liquidity and broaden the number of trading counterparties.

CLS group of companies

CLS Group Holdings AG is the company owned by our shareholders.

It was formed to create, develop and provide the operations, technical and regulatory resources needed to provide the 'continuous linked settlement' system.

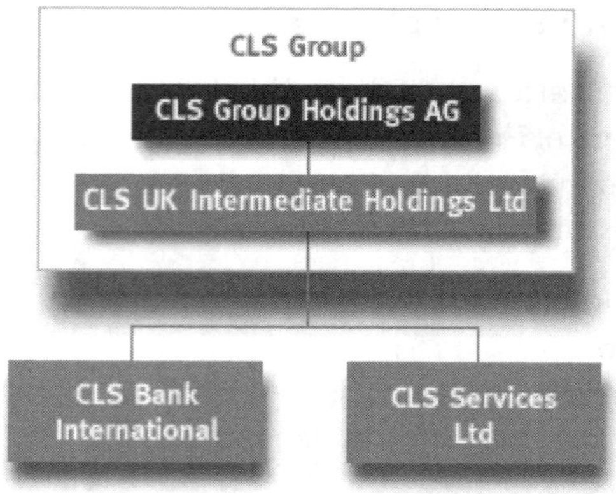

Within the Group are:

CLS Group Holdings AG (CLS Group Holdings)

CLS Group Holdings is the group holding company of CLS UK Intermediate Holdings Ltd, CLS Bank International (CLS Bank) and CLS Services Ltd. CLS Group Holdings is a company incorporated under the laws of Switzerland and is regulated by the Federal Reserve as a bank holding company in the United States.

CLS UK Intermediate Holdings Ltd (CLS UK Intermediate Holdings)

CLS UK Intermediate Holdings is the intermediate holding company of the CLS Group and is a limited company incorporated under the laws of England and Wales. CLS UK Intermediate Holdings is a 'shell' company from a governance perspective and its principal role is to provide certain corporate services to CLS Bank and its affiliated companies (ie Finance, Human Resources, Audit and Communications).

CLS Bank International

CLS Bank is a unique, independent financial institution that provides payment versus payment settlement for payment instructions arising from FX transactions in eligible currencies. It is a wholly owned subsidiary of CLS UK Intermediate Holdings. CLS Bank is an Edge corporation organised under the laws of the United States and regulated by the Federal Reserve Bank of New York.

CLS Services Ltd

CLS Services is a limited company incorporated under laws of England and Wales. The principal role of CLS Services is to provide effective operational and back-office support to CLS Bank and its affiliated companies.

Appendix 4: ISSA recommendations 2000

Recommendations 2000

Status Report 2001

ISSA

INTERNATIONAL SECURITIES SERVICES ASSOCIATION

ISSA Sponsors:

CITIBANK Deutsche Bank Dresdner Bank HSBC
JPMorgan NOMURA UBS

ISSA Recommendations 2000
Status Report 2001

Published by the International Securities Services Association ISSA, April 2002. Printed in Switzerland by NZZ Fretz AG, Zurich.

Contact:

International Securities Services Association ISSA
c/o UBS AG
FNNA OW6F
P.O. Box
8098 Zurich, Switzerland

Phone +41 1 235 74 21
Fax +41 1 236 14 74
issa@issanet.org
www.issanet.org

International Securities Services Association ISSA

The general objectives of the Association are:

- to promote progress and transparency in the securities services industry
- to open communication channels between and develop personal contacts among securities services providers
- to increase the professional knowledge of securities industry participants and the investment community
- to work together with other financial sector industry organisations

This report was authored by the ISSA executive board. At the time of publication of the report, the board was composed as follows:

Sponsor Representatives:

Josef Landolt	Managing Director UBS AG, Zurich (ISSA Chairman)
Raymond A. Parodi	Managing Director Citibank N.A., New York (ISSA Vice Chairman)
Neil T. Henderson	Senior Vice President JP Morgan, New York
John S. Gubert	Head of Group Securities Services HSBC Holdings plc, London
Siegfried Heissel	Senior Manager Dresdner Bank AG, Frankfurt
Andrew D. Carter	Director, Global Securities Services Deutsche Bank AG, Frankfurt
Fuminori Miura	Deputy General Manager Nomura Securities Co., Ltd., Tokyo
Urs Stähli	Managing Director UBS AG, Zurich (ISSA Secretary)

Regional Forum Chairpersons:

Judith Smith	Managing Director Morgan Stanley, New York
Jacques-Philippe Marson	President and Chief Executive Officer BNP Paribas Securities Services, Paris
Wal Reisch	Executive Vice President, Clearing Hong Kong Exchanges and Clearing Limited, Hong Kong

Recommendations 2000

Status Report 2001

INDEX

1. Introduction

1.1 Objectives of this Report

The ISSA Recommendations, published in 2000, are intended to make markets safer, more transparent and more efficient. They cover legal and regulatory frameworks, the effective and efficient use of technology and the maintenance of high standards of operational performance. These are the key areas that the ISSA membership sees as critical for development work in our increasingly global asset servicing industry. These issues need to be addressed by each country or region if we are to maintain the industry's momentum and achieve further progress over the next five years.

This report presents the results of an independent, user driven survey, which ISSA facilitated during 2001, following publication and distribution of the recommendations in the previous year. It evaluates each country's status against both the spirit and letter of the ISSA Recommendations 2000. It identifies the major priorities of the ISSA membership as they work with the different markets to improve the risk profile, competitiveness and efficiency of the different infrastructures around the world. This work is the result of a joint effort to which ISSA's members and correspondents in 44 countries contributed on a voluntary basis. Future updates are planned, and it is hoped that this work can be combined with other parallel initiatives undertaken by groups such as G30.

Although much of the basic research is presented in this paper, the individual market profiles themselves have been published separately on ISSA's website *(www.issanet.org)* due to their size. They are freely accessible to all interested parties.

The information in this report is structured as follows:

This introduction explains the document's objective, the project outline and its working methodology. It also puts the ISSA Recommendations into context with other initiatives that are ongoing at this time.

Section 2 provides an overview of the individual country advances and the most common shortcomings identified in the survey. The shortcomings identified should drive the industry agenda as we move forward.

Section 3 details an action plan and recommendations for prioritisation.

Three appendices complete the report:

- Appendix I: Wording of the ISSA Recommendations 2000
- Appendix II: Notes from the second validators' workshop (November 27, 2001) concluding the 2001 status report.
- Appendix III: Contributing and validating institutions.

The ISSA board is extremely grateful for the support received from the contributing and validating institutions without which this report could not have been completed. We hope that this initiative will make a significant contribution to the development of the global capital market infrastructures, and the service provided to their institutional users and intermediaries, as well as the investor community.

1.2 Overview of the Process

The ISSA Recommendations project was launched in 1999. The ISSA executive board, in consultation with the markets, agreed to a full revision of the nine G30 Recommendations on Securities Clearance and Settlement which were originally published in 1989 and subsequently amended by ISSA.

The first phase of the new project was concluded with the finalisation and ratification of the eight recommendations during the 10th ISSA Symposium in May 2000.

The second phase consisted of their worldwide publication and the subsequent awareness campaign.

This report concludes the third phase in which all ISSA members and some third parties were invited to prepare status reports for their respective local markets, based on a set of 45 key questions. A group of validators, drawn mostly from among the user community (universal banks, global custodians, and broker dealers) within ISSA's constituency, reviewed each market report for completeness and clarity, giving particular emphasis to the needs of the cross-border investor. Where necessary, gaps and areas of conflict were reconciled in a dialogue between authors and validators.
Many of the 45 questions used in the survey cover complex topics. They were deliberately worded in a way as to elicit explanations, rather than simple "check the

box" answers. Hence the ISSA board made a conscious decision to refrain from any attempt to score, rate or rank the markets based on the results of this global survey.

The completed market questionnaires, in their totality, would exceed 550 pages in printed form. Due to the volume, they are made available in electronic format only. As noted above, the market profiles can be accessed on *www.issanet.org*. ISSA have been asked by the validator group to maintain and update this database in the future.

The validators' group was also asked to identify in the markets reviewed areas for potential improvements that would increase transparency, decrease risk, or remove inequality between the treatment of cross-border and domestic investors.

Those items were summarised, cross-referenced to the respective recommendations, and assigned to a logical party to take ownership and action. The resulting document is presented in electronic format on the ISSA website (the "Market Key Issues Schedule"). It is considered by the ISSA board as an integral and significant element of the Recommendations 2000 initiative. However, the board is fully aware that the list cannot claim to be complete, that some of the issues raised may be controversial or may be viewed differently by the respective local markets. It represents, however, the perception of a large group of cross-border market participants. Additions, clarifications, suggestions or comments of any kind are always welcome and encouraged.

ISSA intends to facilitate an ongoing dialogue among all interested parties with regard to the recommendations' subject matter. Where appropriate, new information gleaned from the process will flow into the market profiles, thereby continuously raising their value.

1.3 Relationship Between the ISSA Recommendations and Other Initiatives

ISSA has been a key driver for advances in the post trade securities processing world for many years. Our first review of markets and associated recommendations pre-dates the first G30 report (and indeed was seen by many as the forerunner). It was in early 1988 that the first set of ISSA recommendations was published.

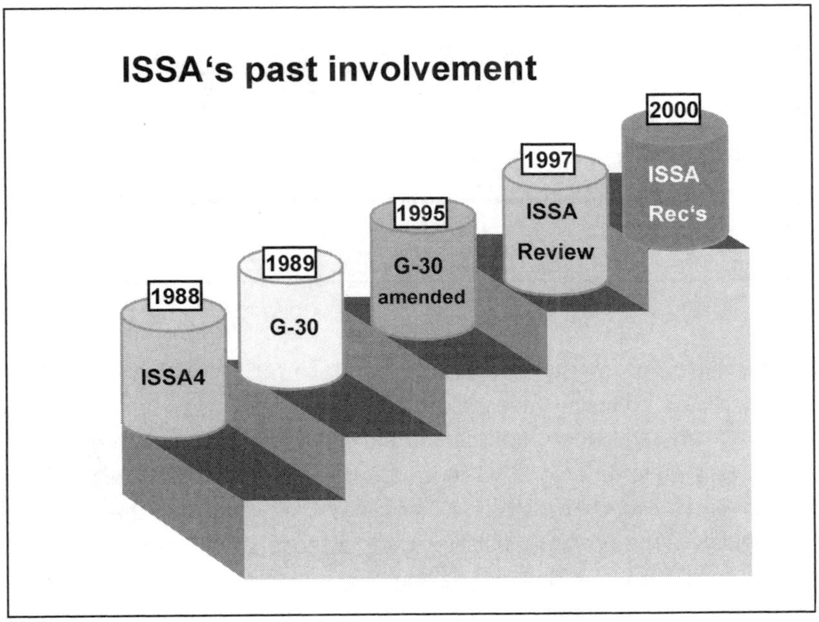

The most recent ISSA recommendations project was launched in 1999. This timing was coincident with similar initiatives of global, regional or sectoral scope but completely independent. Most notably, these are the consultative report on Recommendations for Securities Settlement Systems prepared by the joint BIS CPSS/IOSCO Task Force, and the renewed Group of Thirty effort in clearing and settlement.

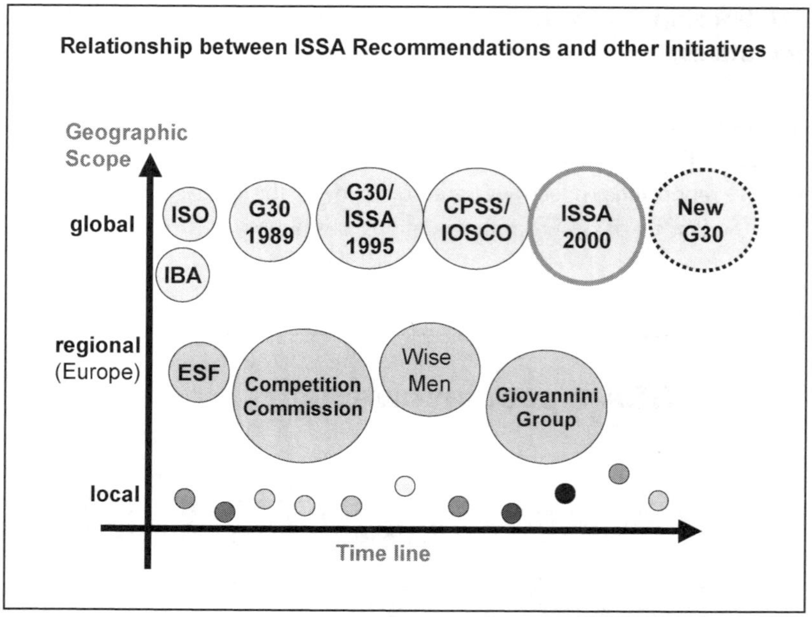

While there is some overlap between the work of CPSS/IOSCO and ISSA, the two initiatives always complemented each other. They share a common goal, namely making markets safer, more transparent and more efficient. However, the focus of each group is quite different. The regulators and central bankers tend to have the stability of entire financial systems in a macro-economic context on their minds. ISSA is not a regulator. The ISSA membership covers a broad scope of market practitioners representing all provider segments along the value chain. ISSA and CPSS/IOSCO became aware of one another's initiative very early on in the drafting stage. The two secretariats met and informally exchanged views and mutual project updates on several occasions.

The G30 report, which is currently in production, is likely to have even greater convergence with the key themes of the ISSA recommendations than the CPSS/IOSCO work. ISSA will have focused more on issues of operational criticality as well as core issues of governance, stability and structure. The G30 is likely to tackle issues from a different perspective, focusing on issues of efficiency, transparency, safety and openness to competition. Several of the key ISSA members involved in the recommendations are also involved in the G30 work. It would appear that the ISSA and G30 works are likely to converge and complement each other. The combined work will be a powerful tool from a broad spectrum of market participants, calling for progress to enable continued growth in capital markets both within countries and across borders.

In Europe, mention should be made of the Giovannini Group, which is advising the European Commission on practical solutions to improve capital market integration in the European Union. The group conducted a comprehensive analysis on the state of cross-border clearing and settlement in the equity, fixed income and derivatives markets in all European Union member countries. Their work looked at the existing infrastructure, governance of the utilities forming that infrastructure, legal, regulatory and tax impediments in today's cross-border operating environment, and the impact of technology. The analysis considers the requirements against which the efficiency of possible alternative arrangements for clearing, settlement and depository services can be assessed. A follow-up report by the Giovannini Group will describe a range of alternative arrangements for an integrated capital market for the European Union. The report is expected to shape the policy making of the European Commission. Although the survey was geographically confined to the European Union member countries, the nature of the issues examined overlaps to a large extent with the scope of the ISSA recommendations. While the Giovannini questionnaire was not addressed to ISSA, many European ISSA members responded to it individually on behalf of their respective institutions.

Looking at initiatives confined to a particular service provider segment within the capital market infrastructure, the Global Association of Securities Clearing Houses (CCP 12) is exploring collaborative opportunities and minimum standards to improve risk management, best practices and process harmonisation for clearing houses and central counterparties. The various regional central securities depository associations have undertaken similar efforts.

ISSA, as noted above, was instrumental in developing the "original" G30 recommendations. It has consistently supported and is now actively supporting, the ongoing G30 initiative. The ISSA executive board is firmly of the opinion that co-operation is vital to ensure clarity of message to the global market place. Diverging or competing sets of best practice recommendations will have a negative effect on market operators. Neither ISSA nor any other organisation in this field should feel proprietary about their work, especially as they often source their value-added knowledge and skill base from similar organisations around the world. Pooling resources and sharing the results among like-minded bodies will enable us all to leverage the existing resources to the advantage of the industry at large. To promote such convergence, the ISSA executive board has therefore formally entered into a dialogue with G30 to seek convergence, and to explore a mutually beneficial form of co-operation.

In addition to the above, work on operational risk being undertaken under the auspices of the BIS ("Basel II") will be monitored as it will impact the allocation of capital to custody and settlement activities.

We also need to monitor the impact of anti money laundering and anti terrorism legislation in several countries as the new mandated controls will require new functionality at infrastructure and user levels and may adversely impact the move to greater Straight Through Processing.

2. Summary and Conclusions

There can be no doubt that the global capital market infrastructure underwent an impressive amount of development and improvement over the last several years. However, the present status survey conducted by ISSA in 44 markets revealed a number of recurring problems or deficiencies as well.

This section summarises the level of compliance with the recommendations, based on analysis of the completed market questionnaires. Further, areas of significant progress and major shortcomings are summarised.

Recommendation 1: Governance

Securities Systems have a primary responsibility to their users and other stakeholders. They must provide effective low cost processing. Services should be priced equitably.

Areas of Convergence and Progress

There is growing evidence of open governance in many Securities Systems with independent user based boards, audit and compensation committees. Most markets indicate that there is no cross subsidisation across instruments, but this is more due to the essentially domestic nature of most CSDs rather than outright policy decisions on this matter.

Increasingly, the Internet is used to relay information to stakeholders alongside newsletters, physical meetings etc. The growing transparency of the market infrastructure towards both its direct and indirect membership is a welcome development.

There appears to be a strong commitment to ensure good communication with the user community in all markets.

Risk or Deficiency Items

In many Securities Systems, stock exchanges and central banks have an important governance role. The depositories are often branches of the trading organisation.

The growth of the concept of exchanges as shareholder value-driven organisations was noted; in some cases these exchanges own the local central depository (monopoly). There is no evidence of user concern at this development in those countries. Examples were provided of possible conflict between the allocation of costs to settlement and custody activities.

> **Recommendation 2: Core Processing**
>
> **Securities Systems must allow the option of network access on an interactive basis. They should cope with peak capacity without any service degradation, and have sufficient standby capabilities to recover operations in a reasonably short period within each processing day.**

Areas of Convergence and Progress

All markets describe their systems as able to handle day-to-day and peak volumes as well as the levels of market volatility experienced in the 12 months of review (approximately from mid 2000 through mid 2001).

Many mature markets described the need to alter their regularly scheduled processing times in the past 12 months as a reaction to problems in the market (e.g. initiated by participants, exchanges, registrars). There are few examples of a market driven outage that led to any material delays. (The events of September 11 in New York post-dated the survey for the USA). The alterations typically are extensions of the regular processing day to ensure orderly settlements within the processing day. This demonstrates the flexibility of the Securities Systems as well as decision-making processes, which meet the needs of the users.

Most securities systems allow interactive access by participants.

Risk or Deficiency Items

Only one market advised of the successful use of their backup/recovery systems in the past 12 months. All other markets have stated that they have not encountered a situation in the past 12 months requiring them to implement their backup/recovery plan.

The industry was very diligent in preparation for the Year 2000 in respect of application systems and in development and testing of validation and recovery processes. Given the World Trade Center tragedy, most markets consider that similar attention and diligence should be applied to ensure that backup/recovery plans are in place and tested for critical systems, procedures and physical sites. However, there is little tangible evidence as to how this is to be achieved. Furthermore, it was noted that there was a special focus needed on the key third party critical points of failure which could include those at major participants, major vendors, data suppliers, telecommunication vendors etc.

100% of the markets responded that their major participants are linked electronically. It is likely that such communication, critical to securities processing, relies on systems/facilities external to the financial services industry. There is clearly a need to consider the backup/recovery plans of key external/third party providers.

Industry organisations and major external vendors on which utility services depend (e.g. in the US: the Securities Industry Association, Futures Industry Association, Bond Market Association), should plan to establish and enforce standards/best practices for backup/recovery of the critical Securities Systems. It is important that these standards be compatible and that they recognise the interaction between different areas of the financial infrastructure.

There is a major need for more openness on contingency plans within each market and across markets. This will ensure that there is greater sharing of best practise and a clearer understanding of the likely impact of any event risk that may arise.

Recommendation 3: Messaging and Standards

The industry worldwide must satisfy the need for efficient, fast settlement by full adherence to the International Securities Numbering process (ISO 6166) and uniform usage of ISO 15022 standards for all securities messages. The industry should seek to introduce a global client and counterpart identification methodology (BIC - ISO 9362) to further facilitate straight through processing. Applications and programmes should be structured in such a way as to facilitate open interaction between all parties.

Areas of Convergence and Progress

Most markets plan compliance with the ISO 15022 standards for message format by November 2002 as scheduled by SWIFT. However, in many cases there is an absence of clear plans as to how this is going to be achieved.

Risk or Deficiency Items

Most markets have local standards for product identification. Few markets, however, have local standards for client and counterpart identification. There is a lack of clarity as to the plans of markets for their moves to ISO 15022. SWIFT has a role through their national advisory groups and best practices process in ensuring that there is clarity in the planning and status of a market given their impact on the different points of connectivity.

SWIFT has a further role as the possible catalyst for the extension of the use of BICs among the non-SWIFT user population. This would need SWIFT members to agree to develop a utility that assigned such codes to all market participants.

There is agreement that standards for messages, product identification and client/counterpart identification are key to achieving straight through processing. Without such standards the full benefits of straight through processing for local and cross border transactions will not be realised and we will continue to process a high percentage of exceptions. Processes developed for cross-border straight through processing (such as GSTP or Omgeo) will promote and to a degree enforce the standards. Shortened settlement cycles will make standards necessary. Market participants should plan to adopt these standards. For many, adoption will include mapping their current local standards to global standards for cross-border activity. Progress is expected to be slow.

Recommendation 4: Uniform Market Practices

Each market must have clear rules assuring investor protection by safeguarding participants from the financial risks of failed settlement and ensuring that listed companies are required to follow sound policies on corporate governance, transfer of economic benefits and shareholder rights.

Areas of Convergence and Progress

Protection Against Delivery Fails or Counterparty Default

Securities lending and borrowing is available without restrictions in most major markets, but is less prevalent in other markets. CSDs typically operate either a centralised service to bridge settlement fails, or facilitate the movement of loaned positions and related collateral where transactions are concluded directly among market participants. A number of markets are in the process of removing barriers which are typically either regulatory or fiscal.

About half of the markets surveyed operate a central counterparty or similar process which enables them to mark failed broker trades to market and collect margin from the failing party to protect the suffering counterparty's interest. The remaining systems have adopted alternative measures to prevent non-performance by a broker, and, in some cases, other counterparties. These include prematching and locking-in of prematched trades, blocking sold shares upon receipt of delivery instructions, strict adherence to the DVP principle, imposition of stiff penalties for non-performance, mandatory buy-in/sell-out, and acting as central counterparty and guarantor. A few markets, both well established and emerging, have no such measures in place, stating no perceived need due to a long history of insignificant fail rates. This approach is questionable given the increased chance of event risk in markets.

Some form of central guarantee fund or compensation fund to protect suffering counterparties has become a standard feature in most markets. However, hardly two markets are alike in terms of where the fund is maintained (exchange, clearing house, CSD, several funds), how it is alimented, to whom it extends (e.g. broker/broker trades or broker/client trades), what instruments it embraces (equities, derivatives, debt), what damage situations it covers (failed trades, counterparty default, loss of securities, misconduct by involved parties, etc.), at what point in time protection sets in (from the moment a trade has matched, from the moment settlement as contracted has failed, etc.), and whether it is supplemented by additional measures such as insurance coverage.

Clarity on coverage and standards on the level and scope of such guarantee funds are critical missing elements.

Transfer of Ownership Rights / Registration

Markets have become increasingly dematerialised and the CSD often acts as registrar, particularly in newer markets. Registration is then performed electronically and is an integral part of settlement. Where registrars are separate from CSDs, they are often linked to the CSD electronically. In a few markets, the function of transfer agent/registrar does not exist; all shares are kept in the (nominee) name of the CSD and participants are responsible for maintaining accurate ownership records. In some markets, registration merely serves to enable shareholders to have the right to vote.

The point in time when the right to entitlements moves from seller to buyer is clearly defined in all markets. In most cases, this occurs at the moment the deal is struck. In a few markets, benefits are vested in the buyer only at the point of settlement, or even registration (which may or may not coincide with settlement completion). At least one major market uses different conventions depending on whether a trade has been dealt on-exchange or off-market.

Corporate Actions and Proxy Voting

Most markets have some level of guidance on the adherence to mandatory time periods between the announcement of a corporate action or other key event, and its completion. Clear legal requirements across the globe, however, exist only with regard to the lead-time between the announcement of shareholders meeting, the meeting date, and the time frame within which dividends must be paid. For other events, guidelines may exist on the level of laws or in exchanges' listing rules, however, rarely on a comprehensive basis. Newer markets tend to be more prescriptive than established ones. While there is clearly no harmonisation of time frames across markets, there is a trend towards addressing the issues in national company acts.

In virtually all markets, issuers are obliged to publicly announce voluntary corporate actions in at least one public newspaper and increasingly to the central market utilities and/or the market regulator. However, issuers are typically neither required to provide information electronically, nor in a standardised format. Standardisation is typically achieved only after the local Securities System or a private sector vendor has reformatted the data for onward dissemination.

As a rule, proxy voting is possible both for local and foreign shareholders in most markets. Rules on whether or not shareholders or proxies are required to be physically present to vote vary by market and often by issuer. Smaller and newer markets tend to require physical presence more often than others do. Voting via Internet is a new development under consideration in a number of markets, already enabled by only a few. In some larger markets shareholder enfranchisement is achieved through "e-voting" which to the extent supported by law, represents an efficient forward looking approach.

Risk or Deficiency Items

Securities lending and borrowing is still not a universally accepted practice; sometimes barred entirely, and sometimes hampered by restrictions. These typically fall into one of three categories, 1) borrowing ceilings or prohibitions imposed on non-resident market participants; 2) tax impediments making securities lending and borrowing economically unattractive; 3) heavy bureaucratic procedures that impede active management of financing requirements.

Cross-border investors' due diligence processes should carefully assess the nature of guarantee funds, the extent of protection they provide, and whether the absence of a guarantee fund may be offset by alternative measures affording equivalent protection. Guarantee funds usually cover on-exchange broker to broker activity, but do not necessarily cover other parties to the transaction flow.

Shareholders need to pay particular attention to the registration practice in all markets where they invest. There are markets where shareholder records are updated only shortly before a record date. This may entail the risk of being informed of problems in a timeframe within which it is too late to take action; particularly where a market has foreign ownership limitations in force and a ceiling has been reached. Inability to collect entitlements or participate in corporate actions may be the consequence.

There is a serious lack of consistency in „cum" versus „ex" trading rules and institutionalised mechanisms to resolve entitlement claims between counterparties. There is also no consistency in the degree to which Securities Systems offer automatic compensation systems, or facilitate the resolution of claims between buyers and sellers.

There is also a lack of harmonisation of lead times in the announcement of corporate actions and their completion, both between different types of actions within a market and across markets. With two or three notable exceptions, markets seem to believe that deadlines to reply to voluntary corporate actions are generally adequate for all investors including those operating through multiple layers of intermediaries. However, the question was frequently not answered and the responses received indicate that local market operators do not perceive this as an issue of concern. Furthermore, there was criticism from the validator group of the lack of adequate time allowed for cross-border investors to respond to voluntary corporate action announcements.

Much corporate action information is available electronically. However, standards associated with the related central databases are not consistent. Neither is the scope of the content of the messages. There are also issues relating to the interpretation of the data and the adequacy of the language and information provided. Dissemination is often via exchanges' websites. However, it is not always accessible to the public at large, or provided in a format suitable for easy onward processing via the industry's established STP tools. Few markets have a truly central and specialised data aggregator and disseminator. The lack of corporate action information and terminology in a consistent format across markets creates the potential for major risk for all parties in the investment flow.

Recommendation 5: Reduction of Settlement Risk

The major risks in Securities Systems should be mitigated by five key measures, namely:

- **the implementation of real delivery versus payment**
- **the adoption of a trade date plus one settlement cycle in a form that does not increase operational risk.**
- **the minimisation of funding and liquidity constraints by enabling stock lending and borrowing, broad based cross collateralisation, the use of repos and netting as appropriate**
- **the enforcement of scripless settlement**
- **the establishment of mandatory trade matching and settlement performance measures.**

Areas of Convergence and Progress

Market settlement periods are generally decreasing. T+1 is being planned for several markets. While most markets generally do not appear to see a move to T+1 as a problem for domestic investors, many are conscious of the need to accommodate the needs of the international investor community. There are markets, however, that did not include the international component although they indicated plans for a change to T+1. Given its impact, the requirements of T+1 must be clearly laid out.

Scripless settlement (book-entry transfer) is becoming the norm although the bulk of markets still utilise immobilised paper. Use of global notes is increasing. The reason for not fully dematerialising typically is of a legal rather than an operational nature. Existing laws often define a security as a "document" or similar term, requiring the existence of a tangible instrument. Comments would indicate that the value of a move to a dematerialised environment is not seen as a priority.

Risk or Deficiency Items

Although there are a series of markets operating BIS Model 1 DvP, the bulk of markets operate Model 2 or Model 3. Few markets have concrete plans to move to Model 1. Some markets have optional use of Model 1, but this option is rarely used. The critical issue for the market is to ensure that there is simultaneity in the exchange of cash and stock in the settlement process and that there is undoubted finality applied to those transfers.

There are many markets with no clear standard on trade matching, especially for indirect market participants. The latter tend to match close to the settlement rather than trade date. It was noted that the driver for trade matching on the market side was regulation (requiring matches at a point close to the trade). On the client side, the driver was settlement date driven. This disparity caused operational friction between different parties.

There was an absence of comment on the use of stock lending and other funding mechanisms as risk mitigation tools. However, most markets enabled turnaround trades and some commented on the right to sell short.

Recommendation 6: Market Linkages

Convergence of Securities Systems, both within countries and across borders, should be encouraged where this eliminates operational risk, reduces cost and enhances market efficiency.

Areas of Convergence and Progress

The majority of Securities Systems have links from the local trading platforms that enable a direct feed of trades through to them to other Securities Systems.

There is growing convergence of infrastructure, but many countries still operate several unlinked Securities Systems. The issue is more one for the OECD and older established markets; emerging markets tend to be equity centric and have addressed this issue.

Risk or Deficiency Items

There are several markets where there are links into the payment mechanism. However, the majority of markets do not link into RTGS systems, either due to the absence of such a system or the preference to use end of day fund systems. Most markets do not appear to be planning such a change.

There is little tangible evidence of commitment to convergence of infrastructure across borders, although there are multiple examples of inter-depository linkages (usually on a free of payment basis).

Recommendation 7: Investor Protection

Regulators in each country should review whether locally domiciled institutions have a process in place that enables them to comply with the laws and regulations of the countries where their investments are placed. In turn, foreign investors should always be treated in like fashion to indigenous investors, especially in respect of their rights to share-holder benefits.

Areas of Convergence and Progress

In a few markets only, regulators actively monitor local custodians engaged in cross-border investments for their compliance with the laws and regulations of the home-market of the investment. Increasingly though, custodians undertake extensive RFP (Request For Proposal) and physical due diligence reviews in order to gather necessary information.

Most markets have some Foreign Ownership Limitations on selected industries of national interest. The process of communicating ceilings and granting benefits on holdings not re-registered varies.

Sales and income proceeds can be freely repatriated in most markets. Markets with repatriation restrictions apply differing and occasionally burdensome procedures.

The number of double taxation treaties concluded between countries keeps steadily increasing, yet the vast majority of countries provide treaty benefits solely through a process requiring a burdensome substantiated tax reclamation.

Risk or Deficiency Items

Information shortage exists due to the fact that few Securities Systems accept the rigours of the Custodian RFP process. The formal nature of individual Global Custodian RFP's can leave gaps as the high risk "grey" areas of many markets may not be adequately explored other than by those agents willing to invest in detailed onsite discovery. This means that some risk issues are not adequately aired and may result in investors and agents having a less than prudent awareness of the rules and regulations in the home market of their investments.

Foreign Ownership Limitation (FOL) processes are very diverse and follow different set-ups. Whereas clearly identified share classes limit the risk upfront, the imposition of limits on undifferentiated share classes carries the risk of becoming aware of a limit problem only after the trade has been made. Further, some markets make the receipt of economic benefits dependent on the successful registration within the FOL ceilings. Investor education and information on these "danger zones" needs definite improvement.

There are several examples of burdensome procedures for repatriation of sales and income proceeds, ranging from registration with the local central bank to a process that results in extensive holding periods prior to repatriation. This constitutes one of major impediments in reaching Straight Through Processing in markets with "exchange controls".

Serious concern continues to be expressed about the difficulty of obtaining best treatment of withholding taxes. Withholding tax procedures are diverse, ranging from straight-forward relief at source payments based on the recipient's address, to requiring extensive documentary evidence involving beneficial ownership disclosure and investor home country tax authority confirmations.

Procedures involving tax reclamation post dividend or interest receipt are more common than upfront relief or exemption situations. Upfront relief situations often result in complex sub-account segregation requirements that may be detrimental to efficient Straight Through Processing in underlying securities transaction settlements. In addition, inconsistency in the application of Double Taxation Treaties in extended custodian chains may lead to differing end-results for the same entitlement.

Recommendation 8: Legal Infrastructure

Local laws and regulations should ensure that there is segregation of client assets from the principal assets of their custodian and no claim is possible on client assets in the event of custodian bankruptcy or a similar event. Regulators and markets, to further improve investor protection, should work:

- **to ensure clarity on the applicable law on cross border transactions**
- **to seek international agreement on a legally enforceable definition of finality in a securities transaction**
- **to ensure that local law fully protects the rights of beneficial owners**
- **to strengthen securities laws both to secure the rights of the pledgee and the protection accorded to client assets held in Securities Systems.**

Areas of Convergence and Progress

In the preponderance of markets, segregation of client assets and participant proprietary assets on the level of the CSD is mandated by law or regulations. In markets where segregation is on a voluntary basis, securities may be either registered in the name of the beneficial owner or the local law assumes that the end investors own the securities. In the latter case, protection of clients' assets in the event of insolvency of a custodian or depository is mainly based on the treatment called for in local bankruptcy laws or from trust and fiduciary laws.

The laws of about half of the markets analysed recognise the existence of beneficial owners who may differ from the legal owner of a security; in some cases this concept is dealt with under fiduciary laws. A fair number of markets do not recognise beneficial ownership and this is a material problem.

Approximately half the markets have clearly defined settlement finality; European Union countries increasingly have adopted the EU Settlement Finality Directive.

Pledgee rights are common in most markets, yet a fair number impose conditions, such as notification prior to executing a forced sale.

Depository loss sharing arrangements often call for a pro-rata liability on the part of participants. In a number of markets depositories resort to insurance coverage, stringent risk management procedures or guarantee schemes. In some important markets, there are no particular guarantee mechanisms in place.

Risk or Deficiency Items

It is clear that a lack of mandatory segregation of assets should not to be regarded as a disadvantage per se, as long as local bankruptcy laws fully protect a client's assets and take the custodian's records as the basis for establishing beneficial ownership.

A lack of recognition of the nominee principle and the distinction between legal and beneficial owner, creates a potential credit risk on foreign custodian banks, in whose name local securities may be registered. They could be considered as beneficial owners and the assets subject to seizure in case of third party claims against such foreign custodians. Resorting to extensive sub-account segregation to avoid this, although possible in some markets, is not cost-efficient.

A clear definition of settlement finality is lacking in too many markets and - where available - not widely known. The time span between custodian settlement notification and ultimate final and irrevocable settlement may expose custodians and their clients to risk.

Home markets with multiple Securities Systems that operate differing finality regulations (usually by way of their rulebooks rather than local legislation) create further risk. Securities Systems should be encouraged to use a common approach or at least to provide sufficient transparency to ensure user understanding of the position.

It is important to note that the issuer or its country of domicile no longer dictates the locus of trade settlement. This means that a single security with a unique ID may be able to be settled in multiple locations. The bulk of market participant processes are not structured to accommodate multiple settlement locations for the same security and work is needed to identify how to tackle this growing problem.

Conditional rights of pledgees are sub-standard in many markets. Avoiding restrictive enforcement procedures in favour of a fast reaction capability would provide an improvement.

3. Action Plan and Prioritisation

Based on the markets' self-assessment supplied by the local contributors responding to the ISSA questionnaire, the validators identified the action plan and priorities detailed below. In coming to their conclusions the validators focused on three key areas of work:

1. The reports submitted by the different markets on their position on the recommendations.
2. The analysis by the ISSA secretariat of the key deficiency items raised in the different countries (as published on the ISSA website).
3. The summary text in Section 2 of this report. This was produced by the board sub group tasked with the monitoring process taking account of input from the validators group.

We provide below our proposed action plan. The plan weighted the different issues and prioritised them according to three criteria, namely scale of risk, complexity of implementation and the number of entities involved or impacted by the recommendation.

Thus, as an example, a recommendation to agree the applicable law to a transaction would be:

- Material in terms of risk reduction as it would enable clarity as to the applicable law in a transaction, which involved cross-jurisdictional impact. This could be through the parties to the trade, the exchanges used to undertake the trade or the intermediary infrastructure used to complete the trade.
- Implementation would be complex as it would require agreement on the applicable law by all the parties involved in the jurisdictions impacted and the enactment of the appropriate legislation in their statute books.
- The number of entities involved would be high as noted above.

The prioritisation would need to be for a term resolution (although this should be in incremental steps and some action could be decided upon immediately) as any other objective could be deemed impractical. The key action points identified as a result of the analysis are explained below to help forward planning and further debate on implementation options.

It was felt though that there were two overarching priorities and these were:

- The need to move forward on corporate actions. ISSA has been a long-term promoter of the use of standard messages in communicating corporate actions. Work is taking place in the USA on the creation of an improved infrastructure to remove the risk of mis-interpretation of a company's announcement by the custodian and broker back offices. Although there will always be unique features to certain complex corporate actions, there is a need to ensure that we enable standardisation of the communications process to the maximum extent possible. Given the work being undertaken in the USA, it would be valuable if the USA shared their work to enable it to be brought for proof of concept in other markets.

- The need to revisit the level of contingency available within the securities settlement systems and the connected infrastructure. This will include the trading environment, the clearing systems, matching environment and the payment systems as well as physical, telephone and other communication structures. There is a need to balance cost and risk. The September 11 events changed the traditional paradigm. For example, there is a need to re-visit the types of contingency systems that may be required to restore operations within a business day. Obviously, contingency planning requires differentiating between high volume and high value systems that create global systemic risk (e.g. major government debt systems which are key to collateral management processes and liquidity management in general) and low volume and low risk systems (e.g. a small equity based market). Last but not least, the issue of providing adequate physical work space for staff to continue/resume work after a disaster event, beyond IT infrastructures and interfaces, needs to be addressed.

Our full analysis shows the following key issues for the markets:

Recommendation 1:

Key areas	Risk impact	Implementation	Breadth of impact
None identified			

Recommendation 2:

Key areas	Risk impact	Implementation	Breadth of impact
• Plans needed to upgrade contingency arrangements for the infrastructure following the lessons of September 11th	Major. Critical to market stability.	Major spend and acceptance by the industry of the cost of the investment.	Material, impacts the entire market.
• It is also important that markets are open about their contingency plans and agree to share experience and best practise.	Material, as such a process helps eliminate the risk of contagion or systemic failure.	Moderate, as it is only sharing of known data.	Moderate, as organisations such as ISSA can facilitate the process.

Recommendation 3:

Key areas	Risk impact	Implementation	Breadth of impact
• Plans needed to ensure market awareness of the move to ISO 15022 in different markets.	Material. Critical to STP.	Material. Needs re-engineering of connectivity by all participants to the Securities System.	Material. Global market issue.
• SWIFT should also agree to offer BICs to non-members.	Material, as it extends standards to all parties.	Simple, as long as SWIFT members agree to give the service their financial backing.	Material. Would extend the reach of STP.

Recommendation 4:

Key areas	Risk impact	Implementation	Breadth of impact
• Improved adherence to global, rather than local, standards.	Important issue. Critical to STP as data quality is a major cause of exception processing.	Material. Impacts all parties to the securities information process from pre-trade through to post trade.	Material impact on the entire market.
• Improved information and standards on the scope of market guarantee funds.	Important issue. Key to assessment of market settlement risk.	Moderate implementation effort. Simple to ensure the clarity needed. Implementation of new standards may lead to restructuring of the funds and may require added capital and/or changed market processes to support them.	Wide impact. Direct participants to all settlement systems (and possibly trading systems as well).

• Proxy voting via the internet.	Important. Enables the implementation of best practise in respect of corporate governance.	Complex, as a distributed environment outside normal constituency of Securities System. Corporate secretaries and local law as well as the creation of the needed infrastructure (can be through the Securities System or by way of the private sector).	Complex. The catalyst for this will best come with the agreement of the corporate sector to embrace and support such an initiative.
• Registration procedures need to be improved (although the ISSA constituency is neutral on dematerialization versus immobilisation).	Material. Common standards will remove risk of any lost entitlements or ambiguity on market claim entitlements.	Moderate. Market rules in each market need to be changed to protect the investor from loss of security or entitlements from the point of trade.	Moderate. Local market issue.
• Standardisation of corporate action information.	Critical. Major area of risk and loss for the market.	Material. Major IT and business project.	Material. Global co-ordination, vendor and market participant issue needing local market co-operation.

Recommendation 5:

Key areas	Risk impact	Implementation	Breadth of impact
• Need to adopt common trade matching standards for both street and market side.	Important. An issue of market rules within the remit of each of the market bodies.	Average. Rule book changes needed and commitment to their implementation.	Moderate. All parties to the trade impacted, but not necessarily systems and workflows.
• Markets need to ensure simultaneity (of cash and stock) and finality in settlement.	Material. Eliminates capital risk at the point of settlement.	Material, as it requires a link between cash and securities systems and also possible legal changes.	Material, as it impacts payment systems and the legislature.

Recommendation 6:

Key areas	Risk impact	Implementation	Breadth of impact
None identified			

Recommendation 7:

Key areas	Risk impact	Implementation	Breadth of impact
• Improved transparency of the rules and regulations for all markets.	Potential high risk although dependent on low frequency adverse event risks.	Moderate. Dependent on information made available by each Securities System.	Moderate. Although transparency could lead to calls for changes in rules and legislation which could be complex.
• Improved structures to enable collection of withholding tax by non-residents.	Moderate risk impact. Creates loss of income to investors.	Complex. Fiscal authorities need to agree market sensitive procedures to enable automation of processes and harmonisation of rules.	Impacts the entire universe of foreign investors.

Recommendation 8:

Key areas	Risk impact	Implementation	Breadth of impact
• Recognition of the concept of beneficial ownership within local laws.	Material. Possible loss of assets by foreign investors.	Complex, as it involves changes to fundamental property laws.	Complex, as it involves regulators and governments.
• Clarity of law of finality.	Material. There is a possible loss of assets by investors in the event of the bankruptcy of another party to the settlement process.	Complex where legal change is needed. Although a simple start would be to define the rules for finality within each settlement system.	Complex, as this involves governments and regulators in the complex area of insolvency law (and often cross border).

Appendix I: Full Wording of the ISSA Recommendations 2000

The ISSA Recommendations 2000 are listed below. A comprehensive document describing the background, explanatory text, monitoring questions and a glossary, was published in June 2000. It is available in hardcopy format (46 pages) from the ISSA Secretariat. A softcopy can be downloaded from ISSA's website *www.issanet.org*.

Note: The wording of Recommendation 7 has been slightly amended from the original version of June 2000. The change has been made due to suggestions received during the second network managers' meeting, and in response to feedback received from many contributors to the first global status survey. (see Appendix II, item 6.)

The recommendations refer to "Securities Systems", these cover depositories, settlement and clearing systems. The term "users" of a securities systems encompasses customers and all other parties to whom the securities system owes a duty of care.

1. Governance

Securities Systems have a primary responsibility to their users and other stakeholders. They must provide effective low cost processing. Services should be priced equitably.

2. Technology: Core Processing

Securities Systems must allow the option of network access on an interactive basis. They should cope with peak capacity without any service degradation, and have sufficient standby capabilities to recover operations in a reasonably short period within each processing day.

3. Technology: Messaging and Standards

The industry worldwide must satisfy the need for efficient, fast settlement by full adherence to the International Securities Numbering process (ISO 6166) and uniform usage of ISO 15022 standards for all securities messages. The industry should seek to introduce a global client and counterpart identification methodology (BIC - ISO 9362) to further facilitate straight through processing. Applications and programmes should be structured in such a way as to facilitate open interaction between all parties.

4. Uniform Market Practices

Each market must have clear rules assuring investor protection by safeguarding participants from the financial risks of failed settlement and ensuring that listed companies are required to follow sound policies on corporate governance, transfer of economic benefits and shareholder rights.

5. Reduction of Settlement Risk

The major risks in Securities Systems should be mitigated by five key measures, namely:

- the implementation of real delivery versus payment
- the adoption of a trade date plus one settlement cycle in a form that does not increase operational risk.
- the minimisation of funding and liquidity constraints by enabling stock lending and borrowing, broad based cross collateralisation, the use of repos and netting as appropriate
- the enforcement of scripless settlement
- the establishment of mandatory trade matching and settlement performance measures.

6. Market Linkages

Convergence of Securities Systems, both within countries and across borders, should be encouraged where this eliminates operational risk, reduces cost and enhances market efficiency.

7. Investor Protection

Regulators in each country should review whether locally domiciled institutions have a process in place that enables them to comply with the laws and regulations of the countries where their investments are placed. In turn, foreign investors should always be treated in like fashion to indigenous investors, especially in respect of their rights to shareholder benefits.

8. Legal Infrastructure

Local laws and regulations should ensure that there is segregation of client assets from the principal assets of their custodian and no claim is possible on client assets in the event of custodian bankruptcy or a similar event. Regulators and markets, to further improve investor protection, should work:

- to ensure clarity on the applicable law on cross border transactions
- to seek international agreement on a legally enforceable definition of finality in a securities transaction
- to ensure that local law fully protects the rights of beneficial owners
- to strengthen securities laws both to secure the rights of the pledgee and the protection accorded to client assets held in Securities Systems.

Appendix II: Summary of Second Network Managers Meeting

The meeting was held in New York on November 27, 2001.

1. Welcome and update on work to date (Judith Smith)

- Since the last meeting in April 2001, 43 out of the 53 market questionnaires have been completed and all but 5 have been validated.
- In today's meeting the draft of the ISSA report will be discussed, and an improved version will be circulated for final edits following the meeting. An action plan will be developed from today's discussion.

2. Group of Thirty relationship with ISSA (Josef Landolt)

- Prior ISSA involvement with the Group of Thirty (G30) has been as follows: In 1988, ISSA developed the ISSA 4 Recommendations which formed the foundation for the G30 Recommendations on Securities Clearance and Settlement Systems in 1989. The G30 recommendations were amended in 1995 by ISSA. ISSA undertook a compliance status update in 1997. In 1999 the ISSA Executive Board conducted a review of the nine G30 recommendations published in 1989. The reviewing process resulted in the finalisation and ratification of the eight ISSA Recommendations 2000, which were published worldwide and were further championed in an awareness campaign.

- Josef Landolt reviewed the relationship between the ISSA Recommendations and other initiatives: European initiatives such as the European Securities Forum (ESF), the Giovannini Group, documentation compiled by the EC Competition Commission and the Wise Men; global initiatives, standards and recommendations such as those published by ISO, the International Bar Association, CPSS/IOSCO and G30. They vary in terms of scope, asset classes and geographic regions covered.

- Many ISSA members have actively contributed towards developing the Recommendations 2000 which were formally approved by the membership during the last ISSA Symposium.

- How will ISSA go forward?
  - G30 plans to publish their recommendations in early 2002. ISSA will continue to work with G30.
  - ISSA will compare and consolidate their recommendations with G30's.
  - A recent conversation with Sir Andrew Large confirmed ISSA's likely role as the monitoring body for the new G30 recommendations.
  - The upcoming G30 Offsite Workshop will have significant representation from the ISSA Board.
  - A comparison matrix of the G30 vs. ISSA Recommendations 2000 (prepared by G30) shows the differences between the current and previous recommendations. They are not substantial.

3. Validation of the Conclusions: Part 2 of the Draft Report (Urs Stähli)

Urs Stähli reviewed the summary conclusion from each recommendation, focusing on a few key issues.

Recommendation 1: Governance:

- Increased evidence of open governance and a decrease in vertical silos.
- Decreased cross subsidisation across instruments.
- Growing use of the Internet (and other electronic means of information distribution) increases transparency of the market place.

Recommendation 2: Core Processing

- As was to be expected, we have seen significant systems development in the past decade.
- Alterations of processing schedules demonstrate flexibility of processing and service providers meeting the needs of their users.

Recommendation 3: Messaging and Standards

- Most markets plan compliance with ISO 15022 but there is no guarantee as to when full compliance will be achieved.

Recommendation 4: Uniform Market Practice

- Protection against delivery or counterparty fails:
  - There are no consistent procedures in securities lending and borrowing across markets.
  - There are no consistencies on how central guarantee/compensation funds are managed or administered.

- Transfer of ownership:
  - The point in time the right to entitlements moves from seller to buyer is clearly defined in all markets. However, there are markets which use different conventions depending on whether a trade has been dealt on-exchange or off-market.

- Corporate actions:
  - There is significant loss potential in current corporate action processing.
  - ISSA has initiated a pilot program, lead by Morgan Stanley, in conjunction with other industry groups, to standardise information distribution methods, timing, etc. The pilot will focus on a few event types in the US in order to prove the concept prior to extending it to other markets and event types.

Recommendation 5: Reduction of Settlement Risk

- T+1 may result in increased operating risk.
- There is a question whether STP is sufficient to achieve the benefits as stated in the US Securities Industry Association's analysis, or whether shortened settlement cycles are also necessary.
- There are mixed opinions on the importance of full dematerialisation as opposed to immobilisation of securities, in order to reduce settlement risk to the greatest extent possible.

Recommendation 6: Market Linkages

- The value of a linkage depends on its features. How much volume does it capture? Is there an incentive to use it? Is implementation - which will almost always cause temporary disruption - worth the efforts and risks?

Recommendation 7: Investor Protection

- The recommendation is intended to address the complex issues of: money laundering, "know your customer", client privacy, voting rights, and double taxation. Its wording has created confusion among many respondents to the first compliance survey conducted by the ISSA Secretariat over the course of this year. The ISSA Executive Board will propose a revision. (Discussed later in the meeting.)

Recommendation 8: Legal Infrastructure

- There are a fair number of markets where depositories resort to insurance coverage, stringent risk management procedures or guarantee schemes. In some important markets, there are no particular guarantee mechanisms in place.

4. ISSA Action Plan and Priorities (John Gubert)

- The slides shown pick up key areas that still warrant discussion.
- The priorities to be spelled out in the report should focus on a 12-18 month time horizon and take into account practicality and what can realistically be achieved.
- Define risk impact
  - Breadth of impact
  - Identify key issues

The final version of the draft table presented in the meeting is included in Section 3 of this report.

Discussion points and conclusions included the following:

Recommendation 1: Governance

- Roles of stock exchanges and central banks in settlement
- Depositories as shareholder value organisations
- Cost allocation between settlement and custody

<u>High priority issues</u>: none identified.

Recommendation 2: Core Processing

- Need for interactive process
- Greater focus on 3rd party critical points of failure

<u>High priority issues:</u> - Proof of resilience of back-up facilities
- Stance on contingency post September 11
- Back-up standards of Securities Systems and major suppliers and key participants

Encourage the markets to be more open with respect to their contingency arrangements. Within ISSA, there should be a dialogue among members on actions being taken in markets. Greater detail is needed for understanding back-up issues. ISSA to start drawing up a list of those issues to tackle. Ask the membership to share the key issues to examine in connection with contingency, back-up standards, and roles to be played by major suppliers and key participants. Which industry organisations in what markets are working on these issues, for their markets?

Recommendation 3: Messaging and Standards

- Need for plans for market convergence to ISO 15022
- Absence of client and counterparty identification
- Continued usage of local standards

<u>High priority issue:</u> Combine standards with interoperability

<u>Action steps:</u> SWIFT to be asked to publish more frequently what infrastructure element plans are on how to move to ISO 15022.

ISSA to inquire with SWIFT on how they allocate BIC; also for non-SWIFT members. (Ray Parodi takes care of this issue).

Recommendation 4: Uniform Market Practices

- Measures required to minimise failed trades
- Protection of buyer for entitlements, especially on cum / ex compensation rules
- Physical presence / absence of voting
- Removal of securities lending restrictions
- More due diligence to determine the value/coverage of guarantee funds and equivalents
- Timing of registration to ensure it does not lag settlement
- Formalising guidelines for timing of corporate actions
- Standardisation of corporate event data

<u>Action steps:</u> Last two bullets seen as high priority issues; being addressed in the USA through an ISSA pilot exercise.

Recommendation 5: Settlement Risk

- Need to ensure overseas investors' needs are represented in planning for T+1
- The criticality of dematerialisation versus the adequacy of immobilisation

<u>High priority issue</u>: BIS Model 1 DVP as an imperative. Simultaneity, finality, irrevocability are the critical issues with regard to the "model" question.

<u>Action step:</u> Definition of interoperability. The GSTPA's etc. proof of concept for interoperability. Reiterate to the industry.

Important item to note: standards to be adopted for trade matching. T+0 for any sort of trade matching plus interoperability among trade matching mechanisms.

Recommendation 6: Market Linkages

- Merger of processing for debt and equities in OECD markets
- Value of linkages cross markets versus merger
- Lack of attention to RTGS links.

<u>High priority issues</u>: None identified

Recommendation 7: Investor Protection

- Distinct share classes versus foreign ownership limitations - must be enforceable without the need to physically segregate
- Exchange controls on financial institutions
- Problems of tax reclamations

High priority issues: None identified to be tackled within the ISSA constituency

Recommendation 8: Legal Infrastructure

- Importance of mandatory segregation
- Lack of nominee structures to protect beneficial owners
- Absent settlement finality

High priority issues: None identified to be tackled within the ISSA constituency

5. Discussion: Did the group miss any issues?

Additional aspects mentioned included:

- Cross border settlement

  The place of settlement needs to be agreed when the trade is made. Standards to address this particular issue need to be created, but this is especially difficult since GSTP has problems with a scripted trade. This issue falls under standards, laws, and interoperability.

- Central Banks changing the capital requirements for banks (credit limits)
  - What is adopted for banks will be adopted by brokers.
  - Capital requirements are changed depending on scope of risk potential
  - This issue should be placed on a watch list since too little is known to make a judgement on its impact.

6. Revisiting Recommendation 7 (Ray Parodi)

Ray Parodi reported that many respondents to the first global compliance survey had asked for clarification of terms, and for guidance as to the exact intent of Recommendation 7. Some of the validators, too, had experienced uncertainties as to the correct interpretation.

Two alternative, improved versions drafted by the ISSA board working group, were presented for discussion. The wording was changed as follows, for adoption with immediate effect:

Recommendation 7 - old	Recommendation 7 - revised
Investor compliance with the laws and regulations in the home countries of their investments should be part of their regulators' due diligence process. Investors, in turn, should be treated equitably in the home country of their investments especially in respect to their rights to shareholder benefits and concessionary arrangements under double tax agreements.	*Regulators in each country should review whether locally domiciled institutions have a process in place that enables them to comply with the laws and regulations of the countries where their investments are placed. In turn, foreign investors should always be treated in like fashion to indigenous investors, especially in respect of their rights to shareholder benefits.*

7. Next Steps (John Gubert)

- Produce notes/minutes
    - Schedule of country key issues to be completed
    - Update draft report and account for final feedback to be submitted by the validators
    - Circulate new draft within one month, offer comment period of another month
    - Final report (booklet and internet version) to be published within the first quarter 2002
- The ISSA Executive Board will continue its ongoing dialogue with G30 to help develop their recommendations and ensure compatibility.

Appendix III: Contributing and Validating Institutions

Contributors to the ISSA Survey

The market profiles used for this report were contributed on a voluntary basis by the institutions listed below, over a period stretching most of 2001. In some cases, the input was the result of a local working party convened by the designated ISSA contact. The ISSA Secretariat does not always know the identities of those additional institutions. We would like to extend our sincere thanks to all contributors whose names may not be included below. Their omission is not intentional.

The market profiles, in their totality, would form a document exceeding 550 pages in printed form. Due to the volume, they are not available in hardcopy format.

Market	Institution(s)
Argentina	Caja de Valores S.A.
Australia	Australian Stock Exchange; The Reserve Bank of Australia; Austraclear Limited; Westpac Custodian Nominees Limited; National Australia Bank Limited
Austria	Oesterreichische Kontrollbank AG
Bermuda	The Bermuda Stock Exchange Ltd.
Brazil	Brazilian Clearing and Depository Corporation
Bulgaria	Central Depository AD
Canada	The Canadian Depository for Securities Limited; CIBC Mellon; Royal Trust
Chile	Depósito Central de Valores S.A., Depósito de Valores
China	HSBC; China Securities Depository and Clearing Co. Ltd.
Colombia	Cititrust SA
Denmark	Vaerdipapircentralen AS; Danske Bank

Finland	HEX plc
France	BNP Paribas Securities Services; CCF
Germany	Clearstream Banking AG; Deutsche Bank AG; Dresdner Bank AG
Hong Kong	Hong Kong Exchanges and Clearing Limited
Hungary	KELER Ltd.
India	Stock Holding Corporation of India Limited
Indonesia	Indonesian Central Securities Depository
Japan	Nomura Securities Co., Ltd; The Fuji Bank, Limited; Tokyo Stock Exchange; Japan Securities Depository Center
Korea	Korea Securities Depository
Latvia	Latvian Central Depository
Lithuania	Central Securities Depository of Lithuania
Luxembourg	Kredietbank S.A Luxembourgeoise; Clearstream Banking
Malaysia	Kuala Lumpur Stock Exchange
Mexico	Citibank Mexico SA
Netherlands	KAS Bank; ING Bank
New Zealand	New Zealand Stock Exchange; National Nominees Limited
Norway	Den norske Bank; Verdipapirsentralen
Pakistan	Central Depository Company of Pakistan Limited
Peru	CAVALI ICLV S.A.
Philippines	Philippine Central Depository, Inc.
Poland	National Depository for Securities KDPW S.A.
Russia	Citibank T/O
Slovenia	KDD Central Securities Clearing Corporation
South Africa	STRATE Ltd.
Spain	IBERCLEAR

Sweden	SEB Securities Services; Swedish Securities Dealers Association; VPC AB
Switzerland	SIS SEGA INTERSETTLE AG
Taiwan	Taiwan Central Securities Depository Co., Ltd.
Thailand	Thailand Securities Depository Co., Ltd.
Turkey	TAKASBANK
UK	HSBC Holdings plc; CRESTCo Ltd
USA	JP Morgan Chase Bank
Venezuela	Citibank NA

Validating institutions

The custody network management teams of the institutions named below, shared the task of reviewing and validating all market profiles. They also identified the list of items that are potential areas of concern to cross-border investors and which would warrant consideration by the local market operators or regulators.

Bank of New York

BNP Paribas Securities Services

Brown Brothers Harriman

Citibank

Credit Suisse Group

Deutsche Bank

Goldman, Sachs

HSBC

JP Morgan

Morgan Stanley

Northern Trust

State Street

UBS

Although the validations were done with professional care, neither the institutions listed below nor ISSA accept any responsibility for the accuracy or completeness of the information in this document.

International Securities Services Association ISSA
c/o UBS AG
FNNA OW6F
P.O. Box
8098 Zurich, Switzerland

Phone +41 1 235 74 21
Fax +41 1 236 14 74
issa@issanet.org
www.issanet.org

ISSA Sponsors:

CITIBANK Deutsche Bank Dresdner Bank HSBC
JPMorgan NOMURA UBS

Index

Stanisław Umiński, Jarosław M. Nazarczuk (Eds.)
Regions in International Trade